THE WRITER'S WAY

By the same Author

THE POET'S WORLD: A poetry Anthology for Senior Forms.

THE CRITICAL SENSE

TEACHING POETRY

UNDERSTANDING POETRY

THE WRITER'S WAY

AN ANTHOLOGY OF
ENGLISH PROSE

CHOSEN AND EDITED BY

JAMES REEVES

M.A.

1967

CHATTO & WINDUS

LONDON

Published by
Chatto & Windus (Educational) Ltd
42 William IV Street
London WC2
*
Clarke, Irwin & Co Ltd
Toronto

TO

THE STAFF

AND STUDENTS

AT

EASTBOURNE TRAINING COLLEGE

First Published 1948
Reprinted 1954, 1956, 1959, 1961, 1964, 1967

INTRODUCTION

THE main purpose of this book is to help boys and girls of upper forms to write good English. They may try to do this by learning rules and maxims, or they may do it the writer's way—by studying the writing of others. The writer's way of learning his trade is that of intelligent imitation. This anthology contains a series of passages by English prose writers from the fourteenth century to the twentieth, covering a wide range of style and subject-matter, worthy of intensive study, and short enough for this purpose. The essays in a standard collection are often too long for the convenience of class-room study. On the other hand, a collection of short passages may easily become a mere assortment of disconnected " snippets ". This danger has been avoided by the arrangement of the extracts in groups dealing with similar subject-matter treated in different styles or from contrasting points of view.

These principles have guided the choice of passages. Each was to be complete in itself and interesting both in content and in style. The attention of young readers is naturally held by interesting subject-matter above all, yet this book will have failed if it does not help to direct their interest to the question of *how* an author writes as well as of what he writes. Secondly, nothing was to be included that was above the heads of a Fourth Form or beneath the notice of a Sixth Form. Some of the material in the last section may be rather difficult of comprehension, but it was felt to be essential to lead the attention of the reader from the study of things and people to that of ideas. Since the extracts have been arranged more or less in order of difficulty, it should be possible for either a Fourth, a Fifth or a Sixth Form to use the book without meeting unsuitable material, In particular, it is hoped that the book may recommend itself as a companion to English studies in Sixth Forms following a non-literary course. For happily, nobody now thinks it right that science students should pursue exclusively the narrow discipline of their special subjects. Thirdly, nothing has been included or excluded merely because it is familiar or unfamiliar, or because its author is famous or obscure. Thus much of the material will be unfamiliar; while no apology is offered for several passages which happen to be very well known.

Moreover, an anthology of this kind should be capable, as occasion arises, of use as a companion to the historical study of English prose. For this purpose a chronological index is included. Not many extracts of a date earlier than Dryden are included, because it is the later writers who are of the greatest help to present-day students. Enough is given, however, to provide some idea of how English was written at any time from the fourteenth century onwards. Every period is represented, but not every great writer could be included.

It was hoped to make a book which should be in itself a pleasure to read, so editorial notes and comments have been kept to the end. It was felt better not to accompany each passage with set exercises which might or might not be what the teacher wanted. At the same time, the Notes, the Index of references and the suggestions for original work which these contain are an integral part of the book. The Index especially will, it is hoped, prove useful in helping the reader to base his own composition work on a study of the extracts. It should be realised that, while imitation is the basis of composition, *active* study—involving a collaboration between teacher and learner—is the only way of ensuring intelligent and purposeful self-development in the art of writing.

I wish to thank Dr. J. Bronowski, Mr. William Hargest, Mr. Martin Seymour-Smith, and Mr. Denis White for their kind help.

J. R.

ACKNOWLEDGMENTS

For permission to include passages from copyright books I wish to thank the authors (or their representatives) and the publishers of the following:

A. N. DA C. ANDRADE AND JULIAN HUXLEY, *Earth and Man* (Blackwell); MAX BEERBOHM, *And Even Now* (Heinemann); ARNOLD BENNETT, *Literary Taste* (Cape); WINSTON S. CHURCHILL, *The Dawn of Liberation* (Cassell); W. H. DAVIES, *The Adventures of Johnny Walker, Tramp* (Cape); C. M. DOUGHTY, *Arabia Deserta* (Cape); ROBERT GRAVES, *Count Belisarius* (Cassell); LORD GREY, *Fallodon Papers* (Constable); J. L. AND BARBARA HAMMOND, *The Town Labourer* (Longmans, Green); HENRY LAWSON, *While the Billy Boils* (Cape); " LORD " GEORGE SANGER, *Seventy Years a Showman* (Dent); A. G. STREET, *Hedge Trimmings* (Faber and Faber); GEORGE STURT, *A Small Boy in the Sixties* (Cambridge University Press); JAMES THURBER, *The Middle-Aged Man on the Flying Trapeze* (Harper); VIRGINIA WOOLF, *To the Lighthouse* and *Orlando* (Hogarth Press).

CONTENTS

1. NARRATIVE

II. DESCRIPTION AND EXPOSITION

(1) NATURE

(2) PEOPLE

CHRONOLOGICAL INDEX OF AUTHORS

THE MIDDLE AGES TO THE REVOLUTION

THE NINETEENTH CENTURY

THE WRITER'S WAY

I. NARRATIVE

1

WATER, WATER EVERYWHERE

We travelled two days towards those hills, and still they seemed as far off as they did at first, and it was the fifth day before we got to them ; indeed, we travelled but softly, for it was excessively hot ; and we were much about the very equinoctial line, we hardly knew whether to the south or the north of it.

As we had concluded, that where there were hills there would be springs, so it happened ; but we were not only surprised, but really frighted, to find the first spring we came to, and which looked admirably clear and beautiful, to be salt as brine. It was a terrible disappointment to us, and put us under melancholy apprehensions at first ; but the gunner, who was of a spirit never discouraged, told us we should not be disturbed at that, but be very thankful, for salt was a bait we stood in as much need of as anything, and there was no question but we should find fresh water as well as salt ; and here our surgeon stepped in to encourage us, and told us that if we did not know he would show us a way how to make that salt water fresh, which indeed made us all more cheerful, though we wondered what he meant.

Meantime, our men, without bidding, had been seeking about for other springs, and found several, but still they were all salt ; from whence we concluded that there was a salt rock or mineral stone in those mountains, and perhaps they might be all of such a substance ; but still I wondered by what witchcraft it was that our artist the surgeon would make this salt water turn fresh, and I longed to see the experiment, which was indeed a very odd one ; but he went to work with as much assurance as if he had tried it on the very spot before.

He took two of our large mats and sewed them together, and

they made a kind of bag four feet broad, three feet and a half high, and about a foot and a half thick when it was full.

He caused us to fill this bag with dry sand and tread it down as close as we could, not to burst the mats. When thus the bag was full within a foot, he sought some other earth and filled up the rest with it, and still trod all in as hard as he could. When he had done, he made a hole in the upper earth about as broad as the crown of a large hat, or something bigger about, but not so deep, and bade a negro fill it with water, and still as it shrunk away to fill it again, and keep it full. The bag he had placed at first across two pieces of wood, about a foot from the ground; and under it he ordered some of our skins to be spread that would hold water. In about an hour, and not sooner, the water began to come dropping through the bottom of the bag, and, to our great surprise, was perfectly fresh and sweet, and this continued for several hours; but in the end the water began to be a little brackish. When we told him that, " Well then," said he, " turn the sand out, and fill it again." Whether he did this by way of experiment from his own fancy, or whether he had seen it done before, I do not remember.

DANIEL DEFOE

The Life, Adventures and Piracies of Captain Singleton, 1720

2

THIRST

MY thirst was by this time become insufferable; my mouth was parched and inflamed; a sudden dimness would frequently come over my eyes, with other symptoms of fainting; and my horse being very much fatigued, I began seriously to apprehend that I should perish of thirst. To relieve the burning pain in my mouth and throat, I chewed the leaves of different shrubs, but found them all bitter, and of no service.

A little before sunset, having reached the top of a gentle rising, I climbed a high tree, from the topmost branches of which I cast a melancholy look over the barren wilderness, but without discovering the most distant trace of a human dwelling. The same dismal uniformity of shrubs and sand everywhere presented itself, and the horizon was as level and uninterrupted as that of the sea.

Descending from the tree, I found my horse devouring the stubble and brushwood with great avidity; and as I was now too faint to attempt walking, and my horse too much fatigued to carry me, I thought it but an act of humanity, and perhaps the last I should ever have it in my power to perform, to take off his bridle and let him shift for himself; in doing which I was suddenly affected with sickness and giddiness, and falling upon the sand, felt as if the hour of death was fast approaching. "Here then (thought I), after a short but ineffectual struggle, terminate all my hopes of being useful in my day and generation; here must the short span of my life come to an end." I cast (as I believed), a last look on the surrounding scene, and whilst I reflected on the awful change that was about to take place, this world, with its enjoyments, seemed to vanish from my recollection. Nature, however, at length resumed its functions; and on recovering my senses, I found myself stretched upon the sand, with the bridle still in my hand, and the sun just sinking behind the trees. I now summoned all my resolution, and determined to make another effort to prolong my existence. And as the evening was somewhat cool, I resolved to travel as far as my limbs would carry me, in hopes of reaching (my only resource) a watering place. With this view, I put the bridle on my horse, and driving him before me, went slowly along for about an hour, when I perceived some lightning from the north-east, a most delightful sight, for it promised rain. The darkness and lightning increased very rapidly, and in less than an hour I heard the wind roaring among the bushes. I had already opened my mouth to receive the refreshing drops which I expected; but I was instantly covered with a cloud of sand, driven with such force by the wind, as to give a very disagreeable sensation to my face and arms, and I was obliged to mount my horse, and stop under a bush to prevent being suffocated. The sand continued to fly in amazing quantities for near an hour, after which I again set forward, and travelled with difficulty until ten o'clock. About this time I was agreeably surprised by some very vivid flashes of lightning, followed by a few heavy drops of rain. In a little time the sand ceased to fly, and I alighted and spread out all my clean clothes to collect the rain, which at length I saw would certainly fall. For more than an hour it rained plentifully, and I quenched my thirst by wringing and sucking my clothes.

MUNGO PARK
Travels in the Interior of Africa, 1799

3

GULLIVER'S FIRST EXPERIENCE OF THE LILLIPUTIANS

On the fifth of November, which was the beginning of summer in those parts, the weather being very hazy, the seamen spied a rock, within half a cable's length of the ship; but the wind was so strong, that we were driven directly upon it, and immediately split. Six of the crew, of whom I was one, having let down the boat into the sea, made a shift to get clear of the ship, and the rock. We rowed, by my computation, about three leagues, till we were able to work no longer, being already spent with labour while we were in the ship. We therefore trusted ourselves to the mercy of the waves, and in about half an hour the boat was overset by a sudden flurry from the north. What became of my companions in the boat, as well as of those who escaped on the rock, or were left in the vessel, I cannot tell; but conclude they were all lost. For my own part, I swam as fortune directed me, and was pushed forward by wind and tide. I often let my legs drop, and could feel no bottom: but when I was almost gone, and able to struggle no longer, I found myself within my depth; and by this time the storm was much abated. The declivity was so small, that I walked near a mile before I got to the shore, which I conjectured was about eight a clock in the evening. I then advanced forward near half a mile, but could not discover any sign of houses or inhabitants; at least I was in so weak a condition, that I did not observe them. I was extremely tired, and with that, and the heat of the weather, and about half a pint of brandy that I drank as I left the ship, I found myself much inclined to sleep. I lay down on the grass, which was very short and soft, where I slept sounder than ever I remember to have done in my life, and, as I reckoned, about nine hours; for when I awaked, it was just day-light. I attempted to rise, but was not able to stir: for as I happened to lie on my back, I found my arms and legs were strongly fastened on each side to the ground; and my hair, which was long and thick, tied down in the same manner. I likewise felt several slender ligatures across my body, from my armpits to my thighs. I could only look upwards, the sun began to grow hot, and the light offended my eyes. I heard a confused noise about me, but in the posture I lay, could see nothing except the sky. In a little time I felt something alive moving on my left leg, which advancing gently forward over my breast, came almost up to my chin; when bending my eyes downwards as much as I could, I perceived it to be a human creature not six inches high, with a bow and arrow in his hands, and a quiver at his back. In the meantime, I felt at least forty more of the same kind (as I conjectured) following the first. I was in the utmost astonishment, and roared so loud, that they all ran back in a fright; and some of them, as I was afterwards told, were hurt with the falls they got by leaping from my sides upon the ground. However, they soon returned, and one of them, who ventured so far as to get a full sight of my face, lifting up his hands and eyes by way of admiration, cried out in a shrill, but distinct voice, *Hekinah degul*: the others repeated the same words several times, but then I knew not what they meant.

JONATHAN SWIFT
Gulliver's Travels, 1726

4

THE THAMES FROZEN

THE frost continuing more and more severe, the Thames before London was still planted with booths in formal streets, all sorts of trades and shops furnished, and full of commodities, even to a printing-press, where the people and ladies took a fancy to have their names printed, and the day and year set down when printed on the Thames: this humour took so universally, that it was estimated the printer gained £5 a day for printing a line only, at sixpence a name, besides what he got by ballads, &c. Coaches plied from Westminster to the Temple, and from several other stairs to and fro, as in the streets, sleds, sliding with skates, a bull-baiting, horse and coach-races, puppet-plays and interludes, cooks, tippling, and other lewd places, so that it seemed to be a bacchanalian triumph, or carnival on the water, whilst it was a severe judgment on the land, the trees not only splitting, as if lighting-struck, but men and cattle perishing in divers places, and the very seas so locked up with ice, that no vessels could stir out or come in. The fowls, fish and birds, and all our exotic plants and greens, universally perishing. Many parks of deer were destroyed, and all sorts of fuel so dear, that there were great contributions to preserve the poor alive. Nor was this severe weather much less intense in most parts of Europe, even as far as Spain and the most southern tracts. London, by reason of the excessive coldness of the air hindering the ascent of the smoke, was so filled with the fuliginous steam of the sea-coal, that hardly could one see across the streets, and this filling the lungs with its gross particles, exceedingly obstructed the breast, so as one could scarcely breathe. Here was no water to be had from the pipes and engines, nor could the brewers and divers other tradesmen work, and every moment was full of disastrous accidents.

JOHN EVELYN
Diary, January 24th, 1684

5

THE GREAT FROST

THE Great Frost was, historians tell us, the most severe that has ever visited these islands. Birds froze in mid-air and fell like stones to the ground. At Norwich a young countrywoman started to cross the road in her usual robust health and was seen by the onlookers to turn visibly to powder and be blown in a puff of dust over the roofs as the icy blast struck her at the street corner. The mortality among sheep and cattle was enormous. Corpses froze and could not be drawn from the sheets. It was no uncommon sight to come upon a whole herd of swine frozen immovable upon the road. The fields were full of shepherds, ploughmen, teams of horses, and little bird-scaring boys all struck stark in the act of the moment, one with his hand to his nose, another with the bottle to his lips, a third with a stone raised to throw at the raven who sat, as if stuffed, upon the hedge within a yard of him. The severity of the frost was so extraordinary that a kind of petrifaction sometimes ensued; and it was commonly supposed that the great increase of rocks in some parts of Derbyshire was due to no eruption, for there was none, but to the solidification of unfortunate wayfarers who had been turned literally to stone where they stood. The Church could give little help in the matter, and though some landowners had these relics blessed, the most part preferred to use them either as landmarks, scratching-posts for sheep, or, when the form of the stone allowed, drinking troughs for cattle, which purposes they serve, admirably for the most part, to this day.

VIRGINIA WOOLF
Orlando, 1929

6

CLIMBING MONT BLANC

I now filled our empty wine-bottle with snow and placed it in the sunshine, that we might have a little water on our return. We then rose; it was half-past two o'clock; we had been upwards of twelve hours climbing, and I calculated that, whether we reached the summit or not, we could at all events work *towards* it for another hour. To the sense of fatigue previously experienced, a new phenomenon was now added—the beating of the heart. We were incessantly pulled up by this, which sometimes became so intense as to suggest danger. I counted the number of paces which we were able to accomplish without resting, and found that at the end of every twenty, sometimes at the end of fifteen, we were compelled to pause. At each pause my heart throbbed audibly, as I leaned upon my staff, and the subsidence of this action was always the signal for further advance. My breathing was quick, but light and unimpeded. I endeavoured to ascertain whether the hip-joint, on account of the diminished atmospheric pressure, became loosened, so as to throw the weight of the leg upon the surrounding ligaments, but could not be certain about it. I also sought a little aid and encouragement from philosophy, endeavouring to remember what great things had been done by the accumulation of small quantities, and I urged upon myself that the present was a case in point, and that the summation of distances twenty paces each must finally place us at the top. Still the question of time left the matter long in doubt, and until we had passed the Derniers Rochers we worked on with the stern indifference of men who were doing their duty, and did not look to consequences. Here, however, a gleam of hope began to brighten our souls: the summit became visibily nearer, Simond showed more alacrity; at length success became certain, and at half past three p.m. my friend and I clasped hands upon the top.

JOHN TYNDALL
The Glaciers of the Alps, 1860

7

DESCENT OF THE FINSTERAARHORN

MY guide at length warned me that we must be moving; repeating the warning more impressively before I attended to it. We packed up, and as we stood beside each other ready to march he asked me whether we should tie ourselves together, at the same time expressing his belief that it was unnecessary. Up to this time we had been separate, and the thought of attaching ourselves had not occurred to me till he mentioned it. I thought it, however, prudent to accept the suggestion, and so we united our destinies by a strong rope. "Now," said Bennen, "have no fear; no matter how you throw yourself, I will hold you." . . . .

Our descent was rapid, apparently reckless, amid loose spikes, boulders, and vertical prisms of rock, where a false step would assuredly have been attended with broken bones; but the consciousness of certainty in our movements never forsook us, and proved a source of keen enjoyment. The senses were all awake, the eye clear, the heart strong, the limbs steady, yet flexible, with power of recovery in store, and ready for instant action should the footing give way. Such is the discipline which a perilous ascent imposes.

We finally quitted the crest of rocks, and got fairly upon the snow once more. We first went downwards at a long swinging trot. The sun having melted the crust which we were compelled to cut through in the morning, the leg at each plunge sank deeply into the snow; but this sinking was partly in the direction of the slope of the mountain, and hence assisted our progress. Sometimes the crust was hard enough to enable us to glide upon it for long distances while standing erect; but the end of these *glissades* was always a plunge and tumble in the deeper snow. Once upon a steep hard slope Bennen's footing gave way; he fell, and went down rapidly, pulling me after him. I fell also, but turning quickly, drove the spike of my hatchet into the ice, got good anchorage, and held both fast; my success assuring me that I had improved as a mountaineer since my ascent of Mont Blanc. We tumbled so often in the soft snow, and our clothes and boots were so full of it, that we thought we might as well try the sitting posture in gliding down. We did so, and descended with extraordinary velocity, being checked at intervals by a bodily immersion in the softer and deeper snow. I was usually in front of Bennen, shooting down with the speed of an arrow, and feeling the check of the rope when the rapidity of my motion exceeded my guide's estimate of what was safe. Sometimes I was behind him, and darted at intervals with the swiftness of an avalanche right upon him; sometimes in the same transverse line with him, with the full length of the rope between us; and here I found its check unpleasant, as it tended to make me roll over. My feet were usually in the air, and it was only necessary to turn them right or left, like the helm of a boat, to change the direction of motion and avoid a difficulty, while a vigorous dig of leg and hatchet into the snow was sufficient to check the motion and bring us to rest. Swiftly, yet cautiously, we glided into the region of crevasses, where we at last rose, quite wet, and resumed our walking, until we reached the point where we had left our wine in the morning, and where I squeezed the water from my wet clothes, and partially dried them in the sun.

JOHN TYNDALL
The Glaciers of the Alps 1860

8

TRADING WITH NATIVES

WE were now at a great loss; the natives were civil enough to us, and came often to discourse with us; one time they brought one whom they showed respect to as a king with them, and they set up a long pole between them and us, with a great tassel of hair hanging not on the top, but something above the middle of it, adorned with little chains, shells, bits of brass and the like; and this, we understood afterwards, was a token of amity and friendship; and they brought down to us victuals in abundance, cattle, fowls, herbs, and roots; but we were in the utmost confusion on our side; for we had nothing to buy with, or exchange for; and as to giving us things for nothing they had no notion of that again. As to our money, it was mere trash to them, they had no value for it; so that we were in a fair way to be starved. Had we had but some toys and trinkets, brass chains, baubles, glass beads, or, in a word, the veriest trifles that a shipload of would not have been worth the freight, we might have bought cattle and provisions enough for an army, or to victual a fleet of men-of-war; but for gold or silver we could get nothing.

Upon this we were in a strange consternation. I was but a young fellow, but I was for falling upon them with our firearms, and taking all the cattle from them, and send them to the devil to stop their hunger, rather than be starved ourselves; but I did not consider that this might have brought ten thousand of them down upon us the next day; and though we might have killed a vast number of them, and perhaps have frighted the rest, yet their own desperation, and our small number, would have animated them so that, one time or other, they would have destroyed us all.

In the middle of our consultation, one of our men who had been a kind of cutler, or worker in iron, started up and asked the carpenter, if, among all his tools, he could not help him to a file. 'Yes,' says the carpenter, 'I can, but it is a small one.' 'The smaller the better,' says the other. Upon this he goes to work, and first by heating a piece of an old broken chisel in the fire, and then with the help of his file, he made himself several kinds of tools for his work. Then he takes three or four pieces of eight, and beats them out with a hammer upon a stone, till they were very broad and thin; then he cuts them out out into the shape of birds and beasts; he made little chains of them for bracelets and necklaces, and turned them into so many devices of his own head, that it is hardly to be expressed.

When he had for about a fortnight exercised his head and hands at this work, we tried the effect of his ingenuity; and, having another meeting with the natives, were surprised to see the folly of the poor people. For a little bit of silver cut in the shape of a bird, we had two cows, and, which was our loss, if it had been in brass, it had been still of more value. For one of the bracelets made of chain-work, we had as much provision of several sorts, as would fairly have been worth, in England, fifteen or sixteen pounds; and so of all the rest. Thus, that which when it was in coin was not worth sixpence to us, when thus converted into toys and trifles, was worth a hundred times its real value, and purchased for us anything we had occasion for.

DANIEL DEFOE

The Life, Adventures and Piracies of Captain Singleton, 1720

9

STEALING CABBAGES

JUST before I got into Tutbury I was met by a good many people, in twos, threes, or fives, some running, and some walking fast, one of the first of whom asked me if I had met an 'old man' some distance back. I asked what *sort* of a man: 'A *poor* man.' 'I don't recollect, indeed; but what are you all pursuing him for?' 'He has been *stealing*.' 'What has he been stealing?' 'Cabbages.' 'Where?' 'Out of Mr. Glover, the hatter's, garden.' 'What! do you call that *stealing*; and would you punish a man, a poor man, and therefore, in all likelihood, a hungry man too, and moreover an old man; do you set up a hue-and-cry after, and would you punish, such a man for taking a few cabbages, when that Holy Bible, which, I dare say, you profess to believe in, and perhaps assist to circulate, teaches you that the hungry man may, without committing an offence at all, go into his neighbour's vineyard and eat his fill of grapes, one bunch of which is worth a sack-full of cabbages?' 'Yes; but he is a very bad character.' 'Why, my friend, very poor and almost starved people are apt to to be "bad characters"; but the Bible, in both Testaments, commands us to be merciful to the poor, to feed the hungry, to have compassion on the aged; and it makes no exception as to the "character" of the parties.' Another group of two of the pursuers had come up by this time; and I, bearing in mind the fate of Don Quixote when he interfered in somewhat similar cases, gave my horse the hint, and soon got away; but though doubtless I made no converts, I, upon looking back, perceived that I had slackened the pursuit! The pursuers went more slowly; I could see that they got to talking; it was now the step of deliberation rather than that of decision; and though I did not like to call upon Mr. Glover, I hope he was merciful. It is impossible for me to witness scenes like this; to hear a man called a *thief* for such a cause; to see him thus eagerly and vindictively pursued for having taken some cabbages in a garden; it is impossible for me to behold such a scene, without calling to mind the practice in the United States of America, where, if a man were even to talk of prosecuting another (especially if that other were poor or old) for taking from the land, or from the trees, any part of a growing crop, for his own personal and immediate use; if any man were even to talk of prosecuting another for such an act, such talker would be held in universal abhorrence: people would hate him; and, in short, if rich as Ricardo or Baring, he might live by himself; for no man would look upon him as a neighbour.

WILLIAM COBBETT
Rural Rides (entry for 1826)

10

THE GOOD SAMARITAN

AND, behold, a certain lawyer stood up, and tempted him, saying, Master, what shall I do to inherit eternal life?

He said unto him, What is written in the law? how readest thou?

And he answering said, Thou shalt love the Lord thy God with all thy heart, and with all thy soul, and with all thy strength, and with all thy mind; and thy neighbour as thyself.

And he said unto him, Thou hast answered right: this do, and thou shalt live.

But he, willing to justify himself, said unto Jesus, And who is my neighbour?

And Jesus answering said, A certain man went down from Jerusalem to Jericho, and fell among thieves, which stripped him of his raiment, and wounded him, and departed, leaving him half dead. And by chance there came down a certain priest that way, and when he saw him, he passed by on the other side. And likewise a Levite, when he was at the place, came and looked on him, and passed by on the other side.

But a certain Samaritan, as he journeyed, came where he was: and when he saw him, he had compassion on him. And went to him, and bound up his wounds, pouring in oil and wine, and set him on his own beast, and brought him to an inn, and took care of him. And on the morrow when he departed, he took out two pence, and gave them to the host, and said unto him, Take care of him; and whatsoever thou spendest more, when I come again, I will repay thee.

Which now of these three, thinkest thou, was neighbour unto him that fell among the thieves?

And he said, He that shewed mercy on him.

Then said Jesus unto him, Go, and do thou likewise.

The Authorised Bible, 1611

11

A WALK TO SALISBURY

IN another walk to Salisbury, he saw a poor man, with a poorer horse, that was fallen under his load; they were both in distress, and needed present help; which Mr. Herbert perceiving, put off his canonical coat and helped the poor man to unload, and after to load, his horse. The poor man blessed him for it: and he blessed the poor man; and was so like the good Samaritan that he gave him money to refresh both himself and his horse; and told him that if he loved himself, he should be merciful to his beast. Thus he left the poor man, and at his coming to his musical friends at Salisbury, they began to wonder that Mr. George Herbert, which used to be so trim and clean, came into that company so soiled and discomposed; but he told them the occasion: and when one of the company told him he had disparaged himself by so dirty an employment, his answer was that the thought of what he had done should prove music to him at midnight; and that the omission of it would have upbraided and made discord in his conscience whensoever he should pass by that place; for, "If I be bound to pray for all that be in distress, I am sure that I am bound so far as it is in my power to practise what I pray for. And though I do not wish for the like occasion every day, yet let me tell you, I would not willingly pass one day of my life without comforting a sad soul, or showing mercy; and I praise God for this occasion. And now let's tune our instruments."

IZAAK WALTON
Life of Mr. George Herbert, 1670

12

SHOWMEN AT A FIRE

I HAVE reason to remember that particular Stepney fair, quite apart from the fact that I left it an engaged man, by an exciting incident that occurred.

There was an enormous rope factory on one side of the green, an establishment that extended over a piece of ground running quite into the country, and on the last day of the fair this was suddenly discovered to be on fire. It was just towards dusk when the flames were first seen, and in a very little time they had made tremendous headway.

The excitement was intense, the people flocking from the fair to witness the fire and to render what assistance they could. With the pleasure-seekers went the showmen, one and all, to give what aid was possible, and an extraordinary scene was the result.

There was no time to take off dresses, and amid the flying sparks, and in and about the burning buildings, could be seen clowns, knights in armour, Indian chiefs, jugglers in tights and spangles, rope-walkers in fleshings—in fact, all the characters of the fair in full dress, striving with might and main to combat the flames.

Here would be seen clown, pantaloon, harlequin, and demon passing buckets from hand to hand, while at another point was the feeble parish engine, manned by sweating Saracens, Crusaders, Roman gladiators, and such-like, pumping as though their very lives depended on their exertions. Up on the building, running along beams with crowbars and hatchets, were the tight-rope walkers, vaulters and acrobats, whose training enabled them to go where no other persons could possibly have clambered, breaking away roofs and walls to prevent the spread of the fire. Over all was the glow of the flames lighting up the faces of the dense multitude that surged and swung and shouted its approval of the efforts of the motley-garbed show-folk to check the advance of the enemy.

It was a picture that would have delighted a painter of weird scenes, though he might have despaired of ever putting its wavering lights and shadows and the strange characters glancing through them effectively on canvas. I know it impressed itself indelibly on my memory, as in my Hamlet dress I took my share of work with the others in checking the roaring flames.

At last our efforts told, and we did check them, but not until enormous damage had been done. A big part of the works was, however, saved, and so pleased were the authorities at the spirit the showmen had exhibited that they gave orders for the fair to continue another day to help make up any losses we had sustained through leaving our booths to become fire-fighters.

We did rare business on that extra day, for the story of the fire had spread, and the public came in crowds to view the scene and to patronise the showmen who had worked so well.

'LORD' GEORGE SANGER
Seventy Years a Showman, 1910

13

A FIGHT WITH A LION

THE Bakatla of the village of Mabotsa were much troubled by lions, which leaped into the cattle-pens by night, and destroyed their cows. They even attacked the herds in open day. This was so unusual an occurrence that the people believed that they were bewitched—'given,' as they said, 'into the power of the lions by a neighbouring tribe.' They went once to attack the animals, but, being rather a cowardly people compared to Bechuanas in general on such occasions, they returned without killing any.

It is well known that if one in a troop of lions is killed the others take the hint and leave that part of the country. So the next time the herds were attacked, I went with the people, in order to encourage them to rid themselves of the annoyance by destroying one of the marauders. We found the lions on a small hill about a quarter of a mile in length, and covered with trees.

A circle of men was formed round it, and they gradually closed up, ascending pretty near to each other. Being down below on the plain with a native schoolmaster, named Mebalwe, a most excellent man, I saw one of the lions sitting on a piece of rock within the now closed circle of men. Mebalwe fired at him before I could, and the ball struck the rock on which the animal was sitting. He bit at the spot struck, as a dog does at a stick or stone thrown at him; then leaping away, broke through the opening circle and escaped unhurt. The men were afraid to attack him, perhaps on account of their belief in witchcraft.

When the circle was re-formed, we saw two other lions in it; but we were afraid to fire lest we should strike the men, and they allowed the beasts to burst through also. If the Bakatla had acted according to the custom of the country, they would have speared the lions in their attempt to get out. Seeing we could not get them to kill one of the lions, we bent out foorsteps towards the village; in going round the end of the hill, however, I saw one of the beasts sitting on a piece of rock as before, but this time he had a little bush in front. Being about thirty yards off, I took a good aim at his body through the bush, and fired both barrels into it. The men then called out, 'He is shot, he is shot!' Others cried, 'He has been shot by another man too; let us go to him!' I did not see anyone else shoot at him, but I saw the lion's tail erected in anger behind the bush, and, turning to the people, said 'Stop a little till I load again.' When in the act of ramming down the bullets I heard a shout. Starting, and looking half round, I saw the lion just in the act of springing upon me. I was upon a little height; he caught my shoulder as he sprang, and we both came to the ground together. Growling horribly close to my ear, he shook me as a terrier dog does a rat. The shock produced a stupor similar to that which seems to be felt by a mouse after the first shake of the cat. It caused a sort of dreaminess, in which there was no sense of pain nor feeling of terror, though quite conscious of all that was happening. It was like what patients partially under the influence of chloroform describe, who see all the operation, but feel not the knife. This singular condition was not the result of any mental process. The shake annihilated fear, and allowed no sense of horror in looking round at the beast. This peculiar state is probably produced in all animals killed by the carnivora; and if so, is a merciful provision by our benevolent Creator for lessening the pain of death.

Turning round to relieve myself of the weight, as he had one paw on the back of my head, I saw his eyes directed to Mebalwe, who was trying to shoot him at a distance of ten or fifteen yards. His gun, a flint one, missed fire in both barrels; the lion immediately left me, and, attacking Mebalwe, bit his thigh. Another man, whose life I had saved before, after he had been tossed by a buffalo, attempted to spear the lion while he was biting Mebalwe. He left Mebalwe and caught this man by the shoulder, but at that moment the bullets he had received took effect, and he fell down dead. The whole was the work of a few moments, and must have been his paroxysm of dying rage. In order to take out the charm from him, the Bakatla on the following day made a huge bonfire over the carcase, which was declared to be that of the largest lion they had ever seen.

DAVID LIVINGSTONE
Missionary Travels, 1857

14

A DOG FIGHT

I RAN across a dim photograph of him the other day, going through some old things. He's been dead twenty-five years. His name was Rex (my two brothers and I named him when we were in our early teens) and he was a bull terrier. 'An American bull terrier,' we used to say, proudly; none of your English bulls. He had one brindle eye that sometimes made him look like a clown and sometimes reminded you of a politician with derby hat and cigar. The rest of him was white except for a brindle saddle that always seemed to be slipping off and a brindle stocking on a hind leg. Nevertheless, there was a nobility about him. He was big and muscular and beautifully made. He never lost his dignity even when trying to accomplish the extravagant tasks my brother and myself used to set for him. One of these was the bringing of a ten-foot wooden rail into the yard through the back gate. We would throw it out into the alley and tell him to go get it. Rex was as powerful as a wrestler, and there were not many things that he couldn't manage somehow to get hold of with his great jaws and lift or drag to wherever he wanted to put them, or wherever we wanted them put. He would catch the rail at the balance and lift it clear of the ground and trot with great confidence toward the gate. Of course, since the gate was only four feet wide or so, he couldn't bring the rail in broadside. He found that out when he got a few terrific jolts, but he wouldn't give up. He finally figured out how to do it, by dragging the rail, holding onto one end, growling. He got a great, wagging satisfaction out of his work. We used to bet kids who had never seen Rex in action that he could catch a baseball thrown as high as they could throw it. He almost never let us down. Rex could hold a baseball with ease in his mouth, in one cheek, as if it were a chew of tobacco.

He was a tremendous fighter, but he never started fights. I don't believed he liked to get into them, despite the fact that he came of a line of fighters. He never went for another dog's throat but for one of its ears (that teaches a dog a lesson), and he would get his grip, close his eyes, and hold on. He could hold on for hours. His longest fight lasted from dusk until almost pitch-dark, one Sunday. It was fought in East Main Street in Columbus with a large, snarly nondescript that belonged to a big coloured man. When Rex finally got his ear grip, the brief whirlwind of snarling turned to screeching. It was frightening to listen to and watch. The Negro boldly picked the dogs up somehow and began swinging them around his head, and finally let them fly like a hammer in a hammer throw, but although they landed ten feet away with a great plump, Rex still held on.

The two dogs eventually worked their way to the middle of the car tracks, and after a while two or three streetcars were held up by the fight. A motorman tried to pry Rex's jaws open with a switch rod; somebody lighted a fire and made a torch of a stick and held that to Rex's tail, but he paid no attention. In the end, all the residents and storekeepers in the neighbourhood were on hand, shouting this, suggesting that. Rex's joy of battle, when battle was joined, was almost tranquil. He had a kind of pleasant expression during fights, not a vicious one, his eyes closed in what would have seemed to be sleep had it not been for the turmoil of the struggle. The Oak Street Fire Department finally had to be sent for—I don't know why nobody thought of it sooner. Five or six pieces of apparatus arrived, followed by a battalion chief. A hose was attached and a powerful stream of water was turned on the dogs. Rex held on for several moments more while the torrent buffeted him about like a log in a freshet. He was a hundred yards away from where the fight started when he finally let go.

JAMES THURBER
from 'Snapshot of a Dog' in
The Middle-Aged Man on the Flying Trapeze, 1935

15

THAT THERE DOG O' MINE

MACQUARIE the shearer had met with an accident. To tell the truth, he had been in a drunken row at a wayside shanty, from which he had escaped with three fractured ribs, a cracked head, and various minor abrasions. His dog, Tally, had been a sober but savage participator in the drunken row, and had escaped with a broken leg. Macquarie afterwards shouldered his swag and staggered and struggled along the track ten miles to the Union Town Hospital. Lord knows how he did it. He didn't exactly know himself. Tally limped behind all the way, on three legs.

The doctors examined the man's injuries and were surprised at his endurance. Even doctors are surprised sometimes—though they don't always show it. Of course, they would take him in, but they objected to Tally. Dogs were not allowed on the premises.

'You will have to turn that dog out,' they said to the shearer, as he sat on the edge of a bed.

Macquarie said nothing.

'We cannot allow dogs about the place, my man,' said the doctor in a louder tone, thinking the man was deaf.

'Tie him up in the yard, then.'

'No. He must go out. Dogs are not permitted on the grounds.'

Macquarie rose slowly to his feet, shut his agony behind his set teeth, painfully buttoned his shirt over his hairy chest, took up his waistcoat, and staggered to the corner where his swag lay.

'What are you going to do?' they asked.

'You ain't going to let my dog stop?'

'No. It's against the rules. There are no dogs allowed on the premises.'

He stooped and lifted his swag, but the pain was too great; and he leaned back against the wall.

'Come, come now: man alive!' exclaimed the doctor impatiently. 'You must be mad. You know you are not in a fit state to go out. Let the wardsman help you to undress.'

'No!' said Macquarie. 'No. If you won't take my dog in you don't take me. He's got a broken leg and wants fixing up just—just as much as—as I do. If I'm good enough to come in he's good enough—and—and better.'

He paused awhile, breathing painfully, and then went on.

'That—that there old dog of mine has follered me faithful and true, these twelve long hard and hungry years. He's about—about the only thing that ever cared whether I lived or fell and rotted on the cursed track.'

He rested again; then he continued: 'That there dog was pupped on the track,' he said, with a sad sort of a smile. 'I carried him for months in a billy, and afterwards on my swag when he knocked up . . . . And the old slut—his mother—she'd foller along quite contented—and sniff the billy now and again—just to see if he was all right . . . . She follered me for God knows how many years. She follered me till she was blind—and for a year after. She follered me till she could crawl along through the dust no longer, and—and then I killed her, because I couldn't leave her behind alive!'

He rested again.

'And this here old dog,' he continued, touching Tally's upturned nose with his knotted fingers, 'this here old dog has follered me for —for ten years; through floods and droughts, through fair times and—and hard—mostly hard; and kept me from going mad when I had no mate nor money on the lonely track; and watched over me for weeks when I was drunk—drugged and poisoned at the cursed shanties; and saved my life more'n once, and got kicks and curses very often for thanks; and forgave me for it all; and—and fought for me. He was the only living thing that stood up for me against that crawling push of curs when they set onter me at the shanty back yonder—and he left his mark on some of 'em too; and—and so did I.'

He took another spell.

Then he drew in his breath, shut his teeth hard, shouldered his swag, stepped into the doorway, and faced round again.

The dog limped out of the corner and looked up anxiously.

'That there dog,' said Macquarie to the Hospital staff in general, 'is a better dog than I'm a man—or you too, it seems—and a better Christian. He's been a better mate to me than I ever was to any man—or any man to me. He's watched over me; kep' me from getting robbed many a time; fought for me; saved my life and took drunken kicks and curses for thanks—and forgave me. He's been a true, straight, honest, and faithful mate to me—and I ain't going to desert him now. I ain't going to kick him out in the road with a broken leg. I—Oh, my God! my back!'

He groaned and lurched forward, but they caught him, slipped off the swag, and laid him on a bed.

Half an hour later the shearer was comfortably fixed up. 'Where's my dog?' he asked, when he came to himself.

'Oh, the dog's all right,' said the nurse, rather impatiently. 'Don't bother. The doctor's setting his leg out in the yard.'

HENRY LAWSON

While the Billy Boils, (First Series) 1924

16

THE KING OF THE CATS

A GENTLEMAN on avisit to a friend who lived on the skirts of an extensive forest in the east of Germany lost his way. He wandered for some hours among the trees, when he saw a light at a distance. On approaching it, he was surprised to observe that it proceeded from the interior of a ruined monastery. Before he knocked he thought it prudent to look through the window. He saw a multitude of cats assembled round a small grave, four of whom were letting down a coffin with a crown upon it. The gentleman, startled at this unusual sight, and imagining that he had arrived among the retreats of fiends or witches, mounted his horse and rode away with the utmost precipitation. He arrived at his friend's house at a late hour, who had sat up for him. On his arrival his friend questioned as to the cause of the traces of trouble visible in his face. He began to recount his adventure, after much difficulty, knowing that it was scarcely possible that his friends should give faith to his relation. No sooner had he mentioned the coffin with a crown upon it, than his friend's cat, who seemed to have been lying asleep before the fire leaped up, saying—'Then I am the King of the Cats!' and scrambled up the chimney, and was seen no more.

P. B. SHELLEY
Journal at Geneva, 1816

17

A TRIAL FOR WITCHCRAFT

HIS lordship[1] had not the good fortune of escaping all business of that kind; for at Taunton-Dean he was forced to try an old man for a wizard; and, for the curiosity of observing the state of a male witch or wizard, I attended in the court, and sat near where the poor man stood. The evidence against him was the having bewitched a girl of about thirteen years old; for she had strange and unaccountable fits, and used to cry out upon him, and spit out of her mouth straight pins; and whenever the man

[1] Sir Francis North: Lord Chief Justice, 1674.

was brought near her, she fell in her fits, and spit forth straight pins. His lordship wondered at the straight pins, which could not be so well couched in the mouth as crooked ones; for such only used to be spit out by the people bewitched. He examined the witnesses very tenderly and carefully, and so as none could collect what his opinion was; for he was fearful of the jurymen's precipitancy, if he gave them any offence. When the poor man was told he must answer for himself, he entered upon a defence so orderly and well expressed as I ever heard spoke by any man, counsel or other; and if the attorney-general had been his advocate, I am sure he would not have done it more sensibly. The sum of it was malice, threatening, and circumstances of imposture in the girl; to which matters he called his witnesses, and they were heard. After this was done, the judge was not satisfied to direct the jury before the imposture was fully declared, but studied, and beat the bush awhile, asking sometimes one and then another questions as he thought proper. At length he turned to the justice of peace that commited the man, and took the first examinations, and 'Sir,' said he, 'pray will you ingenuously declare your thoughts, if you have any, touching these straight pins which the girl spit; for you saw her in her fit?' Then, 'My lord,' said he, 'I did not know that I might concern myself in this evidence, having taken the examination, and committed the man. But since your lordship demands it, I must needs say I think the girl doubling herself in her fit, as being convulsed, bent her head down close to her stomacher and with her mouth took pins out of the edge of that, and then, righting herself a little, spit them into some by-stander's hands.' This cast an universal satisfaction upon the minds of the whole audience, and the man was acquitted. As the judge went downstairs, out of the court, a hideous old woman cried, 'God bless your lordship.' 'What's the matter, good woman?' 'My lord,' said she, 'forty years ago they would have hanged me for a witch, and they could not; and now, they would have hanged my poor son.'

ROGER NORTH
*The Life of Francis North c.*1720

18

SIR LANCELOT AND THE FOUR KNIGHTS

ON the morn Sir Launcelot arose early, and left Sir Kay sleeping, and Sir Launcelot took Sir Kay's armour and his shield, and armed him, and so he went to the stable, and took his horse, and took his leave of his host, and so he departed . . . So Sir Launcelot rode into a deep forest, and thereby in a slade[1], he saw four knights hoving[2] under an oak, and they were of Arthur's court, one was Sir Sagramour le Desirous, and Ector de Maris, and Sir Gawaine, and Sir Uwaine. Anon as these four knights had espied Sir Launcelot, they weened[3] by his arms it had been Sir Kay. Now by my faith, said Sir Sagramour, I will prove Sir Kay's might, and gat his spear in his hand, and came toward Sir Launcelot. Therewith Sir Launcelot was ware and knew him well, and feutryd[4] his spear against him, and smote Sir Sagramour so sore that horse and man fell both to the earth. Lo, my fellows, said he, yonder ye may see what a buffet he hath; that knight is much bigger than ever was Sir Kay. Now shall ye see what I may do to him. So Sir Ector gat his spear and walloped[5] toward Sir Launcelot, and Sir Launcelot smote him through the shield and shoulder, that man and horse went to the earth, and ever his spear held. By my faith, said Sir Uwaine, yonder is a strong knight, and I am sure he hath slain Sir Kay; and I see by his great strength it will be hard to match him. And therewithall, Sir Uwaine gat his spear in his hand and rode toward Sir Launcelot, and Sir Launcelot knew him well, and so he met him on the plain, and gave him such a buffet that he was astonied, that long he wist not where he was. Now see I well, said Sir Gawaine, I must encounter with that knight. Then he dressed his shield and gat a good spear in his hand, and Sir Launcelot knew him well; and they let run their horses with all their mights, and either knight smote other in middes of the shield. But Sir Gawaine's spear to-brast[6], and Sir Launcelot charged so sore upon him that his horse reversed up-so-down.

[1] valley [2] waiting [3] thought [4] fitted in its rest [5] galloped [6] broke in pieces

And much sorrow had Sir Gawaine to avoid his horse, and so Sir Launcelot passed on a pace and smiled, and said, God give him joy that this spear made, for there came never a better in my hand. Then the four knights went each one to other and comforted each other. What say ye by this guest ? said Sir Gawaine, that one spear hath felled us all four. We commend him unto the devil, they all said, for he is a man of great might. Ye may well say it, said Sir Gawaine, that he is a man of might, for I dare lay my head it is Sir Launcelot, I know it by his riding. Let him go, said Sir Gawaine, for when we come to the court then shall we wit[1]; and then they had much sorrow to get their horses again.

SIR THOMAS MALORY
Morte Darthur, 1484

19

DAVID COPPERFIELD'S DINNER

(*At the age of between eight and nine David is sent away by himself to a boarding-school and breaks his journey at an inn to eat the dinner which has previously been ordered and paid for.*)

It was a large long room with some large maps in it. I doubt if I could have felt much stranger if the maps had been real foreign countries, and I cast away in the middle of them. I felt it was taking a liberty to sit down, with my cap in my hand, on the corner of the chair nearest the door; and when the waiter laid a cloth on purpose for me, and put a set of casters on it, I think I must have turned red all over with modesty.

He brought me some chops, and vegetables, and took the covers off in such a bouncing manner that I was afraid I must have given him some offence. But he greatly relieved my mind by putting a chair for me at the table, and saying very affably, "Now six-foot! come on!"

[1] know.

I thanked him, and took my seat at the board; but found it extremely difficult to handle my knife and fork with anything like dexterity, or to avoid splashing myself with the gravy, while he was standing opposite, staring so hard, and making me blush in the most dreadful manner every time I caught his eye. After watching me into the second chop, he said:

"There's half a pint of ale for you. Will you have it now?"

I thanked him and said, "Yes." Upon which he poured it out of a jug into a large tumbler, and held it up against the light, and made it look beautiful.

"My eye!" he said. "It seems a good deal, don't it?"

"It does seem a good deal," I answered with a smile. For it was quite delightful to me to find him so pleasant. He was a twinkling-eyed, pimple-faced man, with his hair standing upright all over his head; and as he stood with one arm a-kimbo, holding up the glass to the light with the other hand, he looked quite friendly.

"There was a gentleman here yesterday," he said—"a stout gentleman, by the name of Topsawyer—perhaps you know him?"

"No," I said, "I don't think——"

"In breeches and gaiters, broad-brimmed hat, grey coat, speckled choker," said the waiter.

"No," I said bashfully, "I haven't the pleasure——"

"He came in here," said the waiter, looking at the light through the tumbler, "ordered a glass of this ale—*would* order it—I told him not—drank it, and fell dead. It was too old for him. It oughtn't to be drawn; that's the fact."

I was very much shocked to hear of this melancholy accident, and said I thought I had better have some water.

"Why, you see," said the waiter, still looking at the light through the tumbler, with one of his eyes shut up, "our people don't like things being ordered and left. It offends 'em. But *I*'ll drink it, if you like. I'm used to it, and use is everything. I don't think it'll hurt me, if I throw my head back, and take it off quick. Shall I?"

I replied that he would much oblige me by drinking it, if he thought he could do it safely, but by no means otherwise. When he did throw his head back, and take it off quick, I had a horrible fear, I confess, of seeing him meet the fate of the lamented Mr. Topsawyer, and fall lifeless on the carpet. But it didn't hurt him. On the contrary, I thought he seemed the fresher for it.

"What have we got here?" he said, putting a fork into my dish. "Not chops?"

"Chops," I said.

"Lord bless my soul!" he exclaimed, "I didn't know they were chops. Why a chop's the very thing to take off the bad effects of that beer! Ain't it lucky?"

So he took a chop by the bone in one hand, and a potato in the other, and ate away with a very good appetite, to my extreme satisfaction. He afterwards took another chop, and another potato; and after that another chop and another potato. When he had done, he brought me a pudding, and having set it before me, seemed to ruminate, and to become absent in his mind for some moments.

"How's the pie?" he said, rousing himself.

"It's a pudding," I made answer.

"Pudding!" he exclaimed. "Why, bless me, so it is! What!" looking at it nearer. "You don't mean to say it's a batter-pudding?"

"Yes, it is indeed."

"Why, a batter-pudding," he said, taking up a tablespoon, "is my favourite pudding! Ain't that lucky? Come on, little 'un and let's see who'll get most."

The waiter certainly got most. He entreated more than once to come in and win, but what with his table-spoon to my teaspoon, his dispatch to my dispatch, and his appetite to my appetite, I was left far behind at the first mouthful, and had no chance with him. I never saw anyone enjoy a pudding so much, I think; and he laughed, when it was all gone, as if his enjoyment of it lasted still.

CHARLES DICKENS
David Copperfield, 1849-50

20

PATRONAGE

To the Right Honourable the Earl of Chesterfield.
My Lord,

February 7, 1755.

I have been lately informed, by the proprietor of *The World*, that two papers, in which my Dictionary is recommended to the public, were written by your Lordship. To be so distinguished is an honour, which, being very little accustomed to favours from the great, I know not well how to receive, or in what terms to acknowledge.

When, upon some slight encouragement, I first visited your Lordship, I was overpowered, like the rest of mankind, by the enchantment of your address, and could not forbear to wish that I might boast myself *Le vainqueur du vainqueur de la terre*;—that I might obtain that regard for which I saw the world contending; but I found my attendance so little encouraged, that neither pride nor modesty would suffer me to continue it. When I had once addressed your Lordship in public, I had exhausted all the art of pleasing which a retired and uncourtly scholar can possess. I had done all that I could; and no man is well pleased to have his all neglected, be it ever so little.

Seven years, my Lord, have now passed, since I waited in your outward rooms, or was repulsed from your door; during which time I have been pushing on my work through difficulties of which it is useless to complain, and have brought it, at last, to the verge of publication. without one act of assistance, one word of encouragement, or one smile of favour. Such treatment I did not expect, for I never had a patron before.

The shepherd in Virgil grew at last acquainted with love, and found him a native of the rocks.

Is not a patron, my Lord, one who looks with unconcern on a man struggling for life in the water, and when he has reached ground, encumbers him with help? The notice which you have been pleased to take of my labours, had it been early, had been kind; but it has been delayed till I am indifferent, and cannot enjoy it; till I am known, and do not want it. I hope it is no very cynical asperity not to confess obligations where no benefit has been received, or to be unwilling that the public should consider me as owing that to a patron which Providence has enabled me to do for myself.

Having carried on my work thus far with so little obligation to any favour of learning, I shall not be disappointed though I should conclude it, if less be possible, with less; for I have been long wakened from that dream of hope, in which I once boasted myself with so much exultation,

My Lord,
Your Lordship's most humble
Most obedient servant,
SAM. JOHNSON.

II. DESCRIPTION AND EXPOSITION

(1) *NATURE*

21

LITERATURE IN DR. JOHNSON'S TIME

NEVER since literature became a calling in England had it been a less gainful calling than at the time when Johnson took up his residence in London. In the preceding generation a writer of eminent merit was sure to be munificently rewarded by the government. The least he could expect was a pension or a sinecure place; and, if he showed any aptitude for politics, he might hope to be a member of parliament, a lord of the treasury, an ambassador, a secretary of state. It would be easy, on the other hand, to name several writers of the nineteenth century of whom the least successful has received forty thousand pounds from the booksellers. But Johnson entered on his vocation in the most dreary part of the dreary interval which separated two ages of prosperity. Literature had ceased to flourish under the patronage of the great, and had not begun to flourish under the patronage of the public. One man of letters, indeed, Pope, had acquired by his pen what was then considered as a handsome fortune, and lived on a footing of equality with nobles and ministers of state. But this was a solitary exception. Even an author whose reputation was established, and whose works were popular, such an author as Thomson, whose Seasons were in every library, such an author as Fielding, whose Pasquin had had a greater run than any drama since the Beggar's Opera, was sometimes glad to obtain, by pawning his best coat, the means of dining on tripe at a cookshop underground, where he could wipe his hands, after his greasy meal, on the back of a Newfoundland dog. It is easy, therefore, to imagine what humiliation and privations must have awaited the novice who had still to earn a name. One of the publishers to whom Johnson applied for employment measured with a scornful eye that athletic though uncouth frame, and exclaimed, "You had better get a porter's knot, and carry trunks." Nor was the advice bad, for a porter was likely to be as plentifully fed, and as comfortably lodged, as a poet.

THOMAS BABINGTON MACAULAY
Encyclopaedia Britannica

22

A VALLEY IN ABYSSINIA

THE place which the wisdom or policy of antiquity had destined for the residence of the Abyssinian princes, was a spacious valley in the kingdom of Amhara, surrounded on every side by mountains, of which the summits overhung the middle part. The only passage by which it could be entered was a cavern that passed under a rock, of which it has long been disputed whether it was the work of nature or of human industry. The outlet of the cavern was concealed by a thick wood, and the mouth which opened into the valley was closed with gates of iron forged by the artificers of ancient days, so massy that no man could without the help of engines open or shut them.

From the mountains on every side, rivulets decended that filled all the valley with verdure and fertility, and formed a lake in the middle inhabited by fish of every species, and frequented by every fowl whom nature has taught to dip the wing in water. This lake discharged its superfluities by a stream which entered a dark cleft of the mountain on the northern side, and fell with dreadful noise from precipice to precipice till it was heard no more.

The sides of the mountains were covered with trees, the banks of the brooks were diversified with flowers; every blast shook spices from the rocks, and every month dropped fruits upon the ground. All animals that bite the grass, or browse the shrub, whether wild or tame, wandered in this extensive circuit, secured from beasts of prey by the mountains which confined them. On one part were flocks and herds feeding in the pastures, on another all the beasts of chase frisking in the lawns; the sprightly kid was bounding on the rocks, the subtle monkey frolicking in the trees, and the solemn elephant reposing in the shade. All the diversities of the world were brought together, the blessings of nature were collected, and its evils extracted and excluded.

SAMUEL JOHNSON
Rasselas, 1759

23

LAKE TANGANYIKA

NOTHING, in sooth, could be more picturesque than this first view of the Tanganyika Lake, as it lay in the lap of the mountains, basking in the gorgeous tropical sunshine. Below and beyond a short foreground of rugged and precipitous hill-fold, down which the footpath zigzags painfully, a narrow strip of emerald green, never sere and marvellously fertile, shelves towards a ribbon of glistening yellow sand, here bordered by sedgy rushes, there cleanly and clearly cut by the breaking wavelets. Further in front stretch the waters, an expanse of the lightest and softest blue, in breadth varying from thirty to thirty-five miles, and sprinkled by the crisp east-wind with tiny crescents of snowy foam. The background in front is a high and broken wall of steel-coloured mountain, here flecked and capped with pearly mist, there standing sharply pencilled against the azure air; its yawning chasms, marked by a deeper plum-colour, fall towards dwarf hills of mound-like proportions, which apparently dip their feet in the wave. To the south, and opposite the long low point, behind which the Malagarazi River discharges the red loam suspended in its violent stream, lie the bluff headlands and capes of Uguhha, and, as the eye dilates, it falls upon a cluster of outlying islets, speckling a sea-horizon. Villages, cultivated lands, the frequent canoes of the fishermen on the waters, and on a nearer approach the murmurs of the waves breaking upon the shore, give a something of variety, of movement, of life to the landscape, which, like all the fairest prospects in these regions, wants but a little of the neatness and finish of Art,—mosques and kiosks, palaces and villas, gardens and orchards—contrasting with the profuse lavishness and magnificence of nature, and diversifying the unbroken *coup d'oeil* of excessive vegetation, to rival, if not to excel, the most admired scenery of the classic regions.

RICHARD BURTON
The Lake Regions of Central Africa, 1860

24

A FOG IN LONDON

It was a cold, dry, foggy morning in early spring. A few meagre shadows flitted to and fro in the misty streets, and occasionally there loomed through the dull vapour the heavy outline of some hackney coach wending homewards, which, drawing slowly nearer, rolled jangling by, scattering the thin crust of frost from its whitened roof, and soon was lost again in the cloud. At intervals were heard the tread of slipshod feet, and the chilly cry of the poor sweep as he crept, shivering, to his early toil; the heavy footfall of the official watcher of the night, pacing slowly up and down, and cursing the tardy hours that still intervened between him and sleep; the rumbling of ponderous carts and wagons; the roll of the lightest vehicles which carry buyers and sellers to the different markets; the sound of ineffectual knocking at the doors of heavy sleepers: all these noises fell upon the ear from time to time, but all seemed muffled by the fog, and to be rendered almost as indistinct to the ear as was every object to the sight. The sluggish darkness thickened as the day came on, and those who had the courage to rise and peep at the gloomy street from their curtained windows crept back to bed again, and coiled themselves up to sleep.

CHARLES DICKENS
Nicholas Nickleby, 1838-9

25

LONDON FOGS

IN a well mix'd Metropolitan Fog, there is something substantial and satisfying—you can feel what you breathe, and see it too. It is like breathing water, as we may fancy the fishes do. And then the taste of it, when dashed with a fine season of sea-coal smoke, is far from insipid.

It is also meat and drink at the same time; something between egg-flip and *Omelette souffle;* but much more digestible than either. Not that I would recommend it medicinally—especially to persons that have queasy stomachs, delicate nerves and afflicted with bile; but for persons of good robust habit of body, and not dainty withal (which such, by the way, never are), there is nothing better in its way. And it wraps you all round like a cloak, too—a patent waterproof one, which no rain ever penetrated. No; I maintain that a real London Fog is a thing not to be sneezed at—if you can help it.

CHARLES LAMB
Essays and Sketches, 1802-1835

26

A STONE AVALANCHE

WHILE we stood pondering here, a deep and confused roar attracted our attention. From a point near the summit of the Weisshorn, a rock had been discharged; it plunged down a dry couloir, raising a cloud of dust at each bump against the mountain. A hundred similar ones were immediately in motion, while the spaces between the larger masses were filled by an innumerable flight of smaller stones. Each of them shakes its quantum of dust in the air, until finally the avalanche is enveloped in a vast cloud. The clatter of this devil's cavalry was stunning. Black masses of rock emerged here and there from the cloud, and sped through the air like flying fiends. Their motion was not one of translation merely, but they whizzed and vibrated in their flight as if urged by wings. The clang of echoes resounded from side to side, from the Schallenberg to the Weisshorn and back, until finally the whole troop came to rest, after many a deep-sounding thud in the snow, at the bottom of the mountain.

JOHN TYNDALL
Mountaineering in 1861

27

A VISIT TO VESUVIUS

VESUVIUS is, after the Glaciers[1] the most impressive exhibition of the energies of nature I ever saw. It has not the immeasurable greatness, the overpowering magnificence, nor, above all, the radiant beauty of the glaciers; but it has all the character of tremendous and irresistable strength. From Resina to the hermitage you wind up the mountain, and cross a vast stream of hardened lava, which is an actual image of the waves of the sea, changed into a hard black stone by enchantment. The lines of the boiling flood seem to hang in the air, and it is difficult to believe that the billows which seem hurrying down upon you are not actually in motion. This plain was once a sea of liquid fire. From the hermitage we crossed another vast sea of lava, and then went on foot up the cone—this is the only part of the ascent in which there is any difficulty, and that difficulty has been much

[1] of the Alps.

exaggerated. It is composed of rocks of lava, and declivities of ashes; by ascending the former and descending the latter, there is very little fatigue. On the summit is a kind of irregular plain, the most horrible chaos that can be imagined; riven in ghastly chasms, and heaped up with tumult of great stones and cinders, and enormous rocks blackened and calcined, which had been thrown from the volcano upon one another in terrible confusion. In the midst stands the conical hill from which volumes of smoke, and fountains of liquid fire, are rolled forth for ever. The mountain is at present in a slight state of eruption; and a thick heavy white smoke is perpetually rolled out, interrupted by enormous columns of an impenetrable black bituminous vapour, which is hurled up, fold after fold, into the sky with a deep hollow sound, and fiery stones are rained down from its darkness, and a black shower of ashes fell even where we sat. The lava, like the glacier, creeps on perpetually, with a crackling sound as of suppressed fire. There are several springs of lava; and in one place it rushes precipitously over a high crag, rolling down the half-molten rocks and its own overhanging waves; a cataract of quivering fire. We approached the extremity of one of the rivers of lava; it is about twenty feet in breadth and ten in height; and as the inclined plain was not rapid, its motion was very slow. We saw the masses of its dark exterior surface detach themselves as it moved, and betray the depth of the liquid flame. In the day the fire is but slightly seen; you only observe a tremulous motion in the air, and streams and fountains of white sulphurous smoke.

At length we saw the sun sink between Capreae and Inarime, and, as the darkness increased, the effect of the fire became more beautiful. We were, as it were, surrounded by streams and cataracts of the red and radiant fire; and in the midst, from the column of bituminous smoke shot up into the air, fell the vast masses of rock, white with the light of their intense heat, leaving behind them through the dark vapour trains of splendour.

P. B. SHELLEY
Letter to Peacock, 1818

28

AN ERUPTION OF VESUVIUS

IN the year 1872 I was a witness of the great eruption of Vesuvius. Standing from the morning alone upon the top of the mountain, that day in which the great outbreak began, I waded ankle-deep in flour of sulphur upon a burning hollow soil of lava: in the midst was a mammel-like chimney, not long formed, fuming with a light corrosive breath; which to those in the plain had appeared by night as a fiery beacon with trickling lavas. Beyond was a new seat of the weak daily eruption, a pool of molten lava and wherefrom issued all that strong dinning noise and uncouth travail of the mountain; from thence was from time to time tossed aloft, and slung into the air, a swarm of half-molten wreathing missiles. I approached the dreadful ferment, and watched that fiery pool heaving in the sides and welling over, and swimming in the midst as a fount of metal,—and marked how there was cooled at the air a film, like that floating web upon hot milk, a soft drossy scum, which endured but for a moment,—in the next, with terrific blast as of a steam-gun, by the furious breaking in wind of the pent vapours rising from the infernal *magma* beneath, this pan was shot up sheetwise in the air, where, whirling as it rose with rushing sound, the slaggy sheet parted diversely, and I saw it slung out into many great and lesser shreds. The pumy writhen slags fell whissing again in the air, yet soft, from their often half-mile high parabolas, the most were great as bricks, a few were huge crusts as flag-stones. The pool-side spewed down a reeking gutter of lavas.

At afternoon, the weight of molten metal risen in the belly of the volcano hill (which is vulcanic powder wall and old lava veins, and like the plasterer's puddle in his pan of sand) had eaten away, and leaking at mid-height through the corroded hill-sides, there gushed out a cataract of lava. Upon some unhappy persons who approached there fell a spattered fiery shower of vulcanic powder, which in that fearful moment burned through their clothing, and, scorched to death, they lived hardly an hour after. A young man was circumvented and swallowed up in torments by the pursuing foot of lava, whose current was very soon as large as Thames at London Bridge.—The lower lavas rising after from the deep belly of the volcano, and in which is locked a greater expansive violence, way is now blasted to the head of the mountain, and vast outrageous destruction upward is begun.

Before the morrow, the tunnel and cup of the mountain is become a cauldron of lavas, great as a city, whose simmering (a fearful earth-shuddering hubbub) troubles the soil for half a day's journey all round. The upper liquid mineral matter, blasted into the air, and dispersed minutely with the shooting steam, is suddenly cooled to falling powder; the sky of rainy vapour and smoke which hangs so wide over, and enfolds the hideous vulcanic tempest, is overcharged with electricity; the thunders that break forth cannot be heard in that most tremendous dinning. The air is filled many days, for miles round, with heavy rumour, and this fearful bellowing of the mountain. The meteoric powder rains with the wind over a great breadth of country; small cinders fall down about the circuit of the mountain, the glowing up-cast of great slags fall after their weight higher upon the flanks and nearer the mouth of the eruption; and among them are some quarters of strange rocks, which were rent from the underlying frame of the earth (5,000 feet lower),—upon Vesuvius, they are limestone. The eruption seen in the night, from the saddle of the mountain, is a mile-great sheaf-like blast of purple-glowing and red flames belching fearfully and uprolling black smoke from the vulcanic gulf, now half a mile wide. The terrible light of the planetary conflagration is dimmed by the thick veil of vulcanic powder falling; the darkness, the black dust, is such that we cannot see our hands, nor the earth under our feet; we lean upon rocking walls, the mountain incessantly throbs under us: at a mile's distance, in that huge loudness of the elemental strife, one cannot almost hear his own or his neighbour's voice.—Days pass and the hidden subterraneous passions slowly expire, the eruption is at an end.

CHARLES M. DOUGHTY
Arabia Deserta, 1888

29

AN EARTHQUAKE

(*The story is told by the servant of Antonina, a lady of Antioch at the beginning of the sixth century.*)

BEFORE giving an account of his exploits, I must tell you a little more about my mistress and myself at Antioch. One day at noon—it was the twenty-ninth day of May—in the year that this new Persian war broke out, we were sitting in the garden porch of the house, waiting for luncheon to be announced. It was a cool place, beautifully tiled in blue, with a perpetually playing fountain and white marble pool, full of vari-coloured fish, surrounded by pots of flowers, some of them very rare ones imported from the Far East. My mistress sleepily held a piece of needlework in her hand, unable to sew because of the oppressiveness of the day; I too was painfully slack-limbed and slack-minded. Suddenly I began to feel sick. The whole earth seemed to heave and rock about me. I was terrified: was it the cholera? Would I die within a few hours? Cholera was raging in the poorer quarters of the city, killing five thousand a day. Not far off stood a magnificent temple in the Corinthian style that had once been dedicated to the Goddess Diana (who is also the Syrian Goddess Astarte), but had now been used for a hundred years or more as the official headquarters of the Blue faction. Looking out through the porch, I tried to steady my gaze on the broad peristyle of this substantial building and its columns of yellow Numidian marble ranked in tall rows. But these too were swaying about in a drunken manner and at a particularly violent lurch they all seemed to topple sideways—and down came the peristyle with a tumble and a resounding crash! I realised suddenly that it was not myself who was sick, but our mother the Earth! What I was experiencing was an earthquake of immense and horrible violence. I snatched up my mistress's boy Photius and her little Martha, who had been playing on the floor near me, and ran out into the garden, my mistress stumbling after me. We were only just in time: a still more violent heaving of the earth flung us all to the ground, and with a roar our beautiful, costly, comfortable house collapsed into a confused mass of rubble and broken timber. Some flying object struck my head and I found myself automatically making swimming motions with my arms, as if I had been flung into the sea from a wrecked ship and was being overwhelmed by hugely swelling waves. Indeed at every moment, though I did not know it, many thousands of my fellow-citizens were swimming too, and in desperate earnest. For the great river Orontes, swollen with its spring flood, had been driven out of its course by the convulsions of the earth; and now swept through the lower city to a height of twenty feet, carrying all before it.

When my head cleared a little, I caught at my mistress's hand and we ran back to where the house had been, frantically calling the names of the two elder children, and the names of their tutor and of the other domestics. But all were buried under the dusty ruins, except for two gardeners, and a footman who had rushed out of the back door when the first shock was felt, and one badly injured maid. We tried to free someone who was groaning close to us in the ruins—I think it was my mistress's sister-in-law—but a sudden wind blew up, and a fire spread through the shattered mass, making rescue-work impossible. Once I thought I heard my mistress's elder boy screaming; but when I went to the spot I could near nothing. After this the shocks gradually diminished in violence. A few hours later we were able to reckon up the day's horrors.

ROBERT GRAVES
Count Belisarius, 1938

30

WINTER ON SPITZBERGEN

No description can give an adequate idea of the intense rigour of the six-months winter in this part of the world. Stones crack with the noise of thunder; in a crowded hut the breath of its occupants will fall in flakes of snow; wine and spirits turn to ice; the snow burns like caustic; if iron touches the flesh it brings the skin away with it; the soles of your stockings may be burnt off your feet before you feel the slightest warmth from the fire; linen taken out of boiling water instantly stiffens to the consistency of a wooden board; and heated stones will not prevent the sheets of the bed from freezing. If these are the effects of the climate within an air-tight, fire-warmed, crowded hut, what must they be among the dark, storm-lashed, mountain peaks outside!

LORD DUFFERIN
Letters from High Latitudes, 1856-7

31

THE SILENT HAVEN

It was one o'clock in the morning of the 6th of August, 1856, that, after having been eleven days at sea, we came to an anchor in the silent haven of English Bay, *Spitzbergen*.

And now, how shall I give you an idea of the wonderful panorama in the midst of which we found ourselves? I think perhaps, its most striking feature was the stillness—and deadness—and impassability of this new world: ice, and rock, and water surrounded us; not a sound of any kind interrupted the silence; the sea did not break upon the shore; no bird or any living thing was visible; the midnight sun—by this time muffled in a transparent mist—shed an awful mysterious lustre on glacier and mountain; no atom of vegetation gave token of the earth's vitality; a universal numbness and dumbness seemed to pervade the solitude. I suppose in scarcely any other part of the world is this appearance of deadness so strikingly exhibited. On the stillest summer day in England there is always perceptible an undertone of life thrilling through the atmosphere; and though no breeze should stir a single leaf, yet—in default of motion—there is always a sense of growth; but here not so much as a blade of grass was to be seen on the sides of the bald excoriated hills. Primeval rocks—and eternal ice—constitute the landscape.

LORD DUFFERIN
Letters from High Latitudes, 1856-7

32

A DESERTED HOUSE

THE house was left; the house was deserted. It was left like a shell on a sandhill to fill with dry salt grains now that life had left it. The long night seemed to have set in; the trifling airs, nibbling, the clammy breaths, fumbling, seemed to have triumphed. The saucepan had rusted and the mat decayed. Toads had nosed their way in. Idly, aimlessly, the swaying shawl swung to and fro. A thistle thrust itself between the tiles in the larder. The swallows nested in the drawing-room; the floor was strewn with straw; the plaster fell in shovelfuls; rafters were laid bare; rats carried off this and that to gnaw behind the wainscots. Tortoise-shell butterflies burst from the chrysalis and pattered their life out on the window-pane. Poppies sowed themselves among the dahlias; the lawn waved with long grass; giant artichokes towered among roses; a fringed carnation flowered among the cabbages; while the gentle tapping of a weed at the window had become, on winters' nights, a drumming from sturdy trees and thorned briars which made the whole room green in summer.

VIRGINIA WOOLF
To the Lighthouse, 1927

33

THE GOOSEBERRY BUSH

THERE be divers sorts of the gooseberries; some greater; others less; some round, others long; and some of a red colour; the figure of one shall serve for the rest.

The gooseberry bush is a shrub of three or four cubits[1] high,

[1] a cubit: about 18 inches.

set thick with most sharp prickles: it is likewise full of branches, slender, woody, and prickly: whereon do grow round leaves cut with deep gashes into divers parts like those of the vine, of a very green colour; the flowers be very small, of a whitish green, with some little purple dashed here and there: the fruit is round growing scatteringly upon the branches, green at the first, but waxing a little yellow through maturity; full of a winy juice somewhat sweet in taste when they be ripe; in which is contained hard seed of a whitish colour: the root is woody, and not without strings annexed thereto.

JOHN GERARD
The Herball or General Historie of Plantes, 1597

34

DAFFODILS

WHEN we were in the woods beyond Gowbarrow Park we saw a few daffodils close to the water-side. We fancied that the lake had floated the seeds ashore, and that the little colony had so sprung up. But as we went along there were more and yet more; and at last, under the boughs of the trees, we saw that there was a long belt of them along the shore, about the breadth of a country turnpike road. I never saw daffodils so beautiful. They grew among the mossy stones about and about them; some rested their heads upon these stones, as on a pillow, for weariness; and the rest tossed and reeled and danced, and seemed as if they verily laughed with the wind, that blew upon them over the lake; they looked so gay, ever glancing, ever changing. The wind blew directly over the lake to them. There was here and there a little knot, and a few stragglers higher up; but they were so few as not to disturb the simplicity, unity, and life of that one busy highway.

DOROTHY WORDSWORTH
Journal for 15*th April*, 1802

35

THE CROCODILE

THE crocodile is a beast that dwelleth in the river Nilus, and his skin is so hard that he recketh not though he be strongly beaten on the back with stones, and layeth eggs in the land that been greater than goose eggs; and his biting is venomous, his teeth been horrible and strongly shape as a comb or a saw, and as a boar's tusk. And no beast that cometh of so little beginning waxeth so great as the crocodile; and is a beast nourished in great gluttony, and eateth right much. And so, when he is full, he lieth by the brink or by the cliff and bloweth for fulness. If the crocodile findeth a man by the brim of the water or by the cliff, he slayeth him if he may, and then he weepeth upon him and swalloweth him at the last.

JOHN DE TREVISA
1326—1402
Bartholomew

36

LAND LIZARDS OF THE GALAPAGOS ISLANDS

LIKE their brothers the sea-kind, they are ugly animals, of a yellowish orange beneath, and of a brownish red colour above: from their low facial angle they have a singularly stupid appearance. They are, perhaps, of a rather less size than the marine species; but several of them weighed between ten and fifteen pounds. In their movements they are lazy and half torpid. When not frightened, they slowly crawl along with their tails and bellies dragging on the ground. They often stop, and doze for a minute or two, with closed eyes and hind legs spread out on the parched soil.

They inhabit burrows, which they sometimes make between fragments of lava, but more generally on level patches of the soft sandstone-like turf. The holes do not appear to be very deep, and they enter the ground at a small angle; so that when walking over these lizard-warrens, the soil is constantly giving way, much to the annoyance of the tired walker. This animal, when making its burrow, works alternately the opposite sides of its body. One front leg for a short time scratches up the soil, and throws it towards the hind foot, which is well placed so as to heave it beyond the mouth of the hole. That side of the body being tired, the other takes up the task, and so on alternately. I watched one for a long time, till half its body was buried; I then walked up and pulled it by the tail; at this it was greatly astonished, and soon shuffled up to see what was the matter; and then stared at me in the face, as much as to say, "What made you pull my tail?"

They feed by day, and do not wander far from their burrows; if frightened, they rush to them with a most awkward gait. Except when running down hill, they cannot move very fast, apparently from the lateral position of their legs. They are not at all timorous: when attentively watching any one, they curl their tails, and, raising themselves on their front legs, nod their heads vertically, with a quick movement, and try to look very fierce: but in reality they are not at all so; if one just stamps on the ground, down go their tails, and off they shuffle as quickly as they can. I have frequently observed small fly-eating lizards, when watching anything, nod their heads in precisely the same manner; but I do not at all know for what purpose. If this Amblyrhynchus is held and plagued with a stick, it will bite it very severely; but I caught many by the tail, and they never tried to bite me.

CHARLES DARWIN
The Voyage of the Beagle, 1839

37

LOCUSTS IN ARGENTINA

AFTER our two days' tedious journey, it was refreshing to see in the distance the rows of poplars and willows growing round the village of Luxan. Shortly before we arrived at this place we observed to the south a ragged cloud of a dark reddish-brown colour. At first we thought that it was smoke from some great fire on the plains; but we soon found that it was a swarm of locusts. They were flying northward; and with the aid of a light breeze, they overtook us at a rate of ten or fifteen miles an hour. The main body filled the air from a height of twenty feet, to that, as it appeared, of two or three thousand above the ground; and the sound of their wings was as the sound of chariots of many horses running to battle; or rather, I should say, like a strong breeze passing through the rigging of a ship. The sky, seen through the advanced guard, appeared like a mezzotinto engraving, but the main body was impervious to sight; they were not, however, so thick together, but they could escape a stick waved backwards and forwards. When they alighted, they were more numerous than the leaves in the field, and the surface became reddish instead of being green: the swarm having once alighted, the individuals flew from side to side in all directions. Locusts are not an uncommon pest in this country: already during this season, several smaller swarms had come up from the south, where, as apparently in all other parts of the world, they are bred in the deserts. The poor cottagers in vain attempted, by lighting fires, by shouts, and by waving branches to avert the attack.

CHARLES DARWIN
The Voyage of the Beagle, 1839

38

A TROPICAL FOREST

On each side of the road great trees towered up, carrying their crowns out of sight amongst a canopy of foliage; lianas wound round every trunk and hung from every bough, passing from tree to tree, and entangling the giants in a great network of coiling cables, as the serpents did Laocoon; the simile being strengthened by the fact that many of the trees are really strangled in the winding folds. Sometimes a tree appears covered with beautiful flowers, which do not belong to it, but to one of the lianas that twines through its branches and sends down great rope-like stems to the ground. Climbing ferns and vanilla cling to the trunks, and a thousand epiphytes perch themselves on the branches. Amongst these are large arums that send down aerial roots, tough and strong, and universally used instead of cordage by the natives. Amongst the undergrowth several small species of palms, varying in height from two to fifteen feet, are common; and now and then magnificent tree ferns, sending off their feathery crowns twenty feet from the ground, delight the sight with their graceful elegance. Great broad-leaved heliconiae, leathery melastomae, and succulent-stemmed, lop-sided leaved begonias are abundant, and typical of tropical American forests. Not less so are the cecropia trees, with their white stems and large palmated leaves standing up like great candelabra. Sometimes the ground is carpeted with large flowers, yellow, pink, or white, that have fallen from some invisible tree-top above, or the air is filled with a delicious perfume, for the source of which one seeks around in vain, as the flowers that cause it are far overhead out of sight, lost in the great overshadowing crown of verdure. Numerous babbling brooks intersect the forest, with moss-covered stones and fern-clad nooks. One's thoughts are led away to the green dells in English denes, but are soon recalled; for the sparkling pools are the favourite haunts of the fairy-humming birds, and like an arrow one will dart up the brook, and, poised on wings moving with almost invisible velocity, clothed in purple, golden, or emerald glory, hang suspended in the air; gazing with startled look at the intruder, with a sudden jerk, turning round first one eye, then the other, and suddenly disappear like a flash of light.

THOMAS BELT
A Naturalist in Nicaragua, 1874

39

NIGHT IN CENTRAL AMERICA

THE night-world is very different from that of the day. Things that blink and hide from the light are all awake and astir when the sun goes down. Great spiders and scorpions prowl about, or take up advantageous positions where they expect their prey to pass. Cockroaches of all sizes, from that of one's finger to that of one's finger-nail, stand with long quivering antennae, pictures of alert outlook, watching for their numerous foes, or scurry away as fast as their long legs can carry them; but if they come within reach of the great spider they are pounced upon in an instant, and with one convulsive kick give up the hopeless struggle. Centipedes, wood-lice, and all kinds of creeping things come out of cracks and crevices; even the pools are alive with water-beetles that have been hiding in the ooze all day, excepting when they come up with a dash to the surface for a bubble of fresh air. Owls and night-jars make strange unearthly cries. The timid deer comes out of its close covert to feed in the grassy clearings. Jaguars, ocelots, and opossums slink about in the gloom. The skunk goes leisurely along, holding up his white tail as a danger flag for none to come within range of his nauseous artillery. Bats and large moths flitter around, whilst all the day-world is at rest and asleep. The night speeds on; the stars that rose in the east are sinking behind the western hills; a faint tinge of dawn lights the eastern sky; loud and shrill rings out the awakening shout of chanticleer; the grey dawn comes on apace; a hundred birds salute the cheerful morn, and the night-world hurries to its gloomy dens and hiding-places, like the sprites and fairy elves of our nursery days.

THOMAS BELT

A Naturalist in Nicaragua, 1874

40

HOMING ROOKS

THE evening proceedings and manoeuvres of the rooks are curious and amusing in the autumn. Just before dusk they return in long strings from the foraging of the day, and rendezvous by thousands over Selborne Down, where they wheel round in the air, and sport and dive in a playful manner, all the while exerting their voices, and making a loud cawing, which, being blended and softened by the distance that we at the village are below them, becomes a confused noise or chiding; or rather a pleasing murmur, very engaging to the imagination, and not unlike the cry of a pack of hounds in hollow, echoing woods, or the rushing of the wind in tall trees, or the tumbling of the tide upon a pebbly shore. When this ceremony is over, with the last gleam of day, they retire for the night to the deep beechen woods of Tisted and Ropley.

GILBERT WHITE
Natural History of Selborne, 1789

41

PIGEONS

A FEW of these may be kept about any cottage, for they are kept even in towns by labourers and artizans. They cause but little trouble. They take care of their own young ones; and they do not scratch, or do any other mischief in gardens. They want feeding with tares, peas, or small beans; and buck-wheat is very good for them. To begin keeping them, they must not have flown at large before you get them. You must keep them for two or three days, shut into the place which is to be their home; and then they may be let out, and will never leave you, as long as they can get proper food, and are undisturbed by vermin, or unannoyed exceedingly by lice.

The common dove-house pigeons are the best to keep. They breed oftenest, and feed their young ones best. They begin to breed at about nine months old, and if well kept, they will give you eight or nine pair in the year. Any little place, a shelf in the cow-shed; a board or two under the eaves of the house; or, in short, any place under cover, even on the ground floor, they will sit and hatch and breed up their young ones in.

It is not supposed that there could be much profit attached to them; but they are of this use; they are very pretty creatures; very interesting in their manners; they are an object to delight children, and to give them the early habit of fondness for animals and of setting a value on them, which, as I have often had to observe before, is a very great thing. A considerable part of the property of a nation consists of animals. Of course a proportionate part of the cares and labours of a people appertains to the breeding and bringing to perfection those animals; and, if you consult your experience, you will find that a labourer is, generally speaking, of value in proportion as he is worthy of being intrusted with the care of animals. The most careless fellow cannot hurt a hedge or ditch; but to trust him with the team, or the flock, is another matter. And, mind, for the man to be trustworthy in this respect, the boy must have been in the habit of being kind and considerate towards animals; and nothing is so likely to give him that excellent habit as his seeing, from his very birth, animals taken great care of, and treated with great kindness, by his parents, and now and then having a little thing to call his own.

WILLIAM COBBETT
Cottage Economy, 1822

42

MOBY DICK

So that, overawed by the rumours and portents concerning him, not a few of the fishermen recalled, in reference to Moby Dick, the earlier days of the sperm whale fishery, when it was oftentimes hard to induce long-practised right-whalemen to embark in the perils of this new and daring warfare; such men protesting that although other leviathans might be hopefully pursued, yet to chase and point lance at such an apparition as the sperm whale was not for mortal man—that to attempt it, would be inevitably to be torn into a quick eternity . . . . .

But even stripped of these supernatural surmisings, there was enough in the earthly make and incontestable character of the monster to strike the imagination with unwonted power. For it was not so much his uncommon bulk that so much distinguished him from other sperm whales, but, as was elsewhere thrown out, a peculiar snow-white wrinkled forehead, and a high pyramidical white hump. These were his prominent features; the tokens whereby, even in the limitless, uncharted seas, he revealed his identity at a long distance to those who knew him.

The rest of his body was so streaked, and spotted, and marbled with the same shrouded hue, that in the end, he had gained his distinctive appellation of the White Whale; a name, indeed, literally justified by his vivid aspect when seen gliding at high noon through a dark blue sea, leaving a milky-way wake of creamy foam, all spangled with golden gleamings. Nor was it his unwonted magnitude, nor his remarkable hue, nor yet his deformed lower jaw, that so much invested the whale with natural terror, as that unexampled, intelligent malignity which, according to specific accounts, he had over and over again evinced in his assaults. More than all, his treacherous retreats struck more of dismay than perhaps aught else. For, when swimming before his exulting pursuers with every apparent symptom of alarm, he had several times been known to turn round suddenly, and, bearing down upon them, either stave their boats to splinters, or drive them back in consternation to their ship.

Already several fatalities had attended his chase. But though similar disasters, however little bruited ashore, were by no means unusual in the fishery; yet in most instances, such seemed the White Whale's infernal forethought of ferocity, that every dismembering or death that he caused was not wholly regarded as having been inflicted by an unintelligent agent.

Judge, then, to what pitches of inflamed, distracted fury the minds of his more desperate hunters were impelled, when, amid the chips of chewed boats and the sinking limbs of torn comrades, they swam out of the white curds of the whale's direful wrath into the serene, exasperating sunlight, that smiled on, as if at a birth or a bridal.

HERMAN MELVILLE
Moby Dick, 1851

(2) *PEOPLE*

43

SIR ANDREW FREEPORT

THE person of next consideration is Sir Andrew Freeport, a merchant of great eminence in the city of London. A person of indefatigable industry, strong reason, and great experience. His notions of trade are noble and generous, and (as every rich man has usually some sly way of jesting, which would make no great figure were he not a rich man) he calls the sea the *British Common.* He is acquainted with commerce in all its parts, and will tell you that it is a stupid and barbarous way to extend dominion by arms; for true power is to be got by arts and industry. He will often argue that if this part of our trade were well cultivated, we should gain from one nation; and if another, from another. I have heard him prove that diligence makes more lasting acquisitions than valour, and that sloth has ruined more nations than the sword. He abounds in several frugal maxims, among which the greatest favourite is, "A penny saved is a penny got". A general trader of good sense is pleasanter company than a general scholar; and Sir Andrew having a natural unaffected eloquence, the perspicuity of his discourse gives the same pleasure that wit would in another man. He has made his fortunes himself; and says that England may be richer than other kingdoms by as plain methods as he himself is richer than other men; though at the same time I can say this of him, that there is not a point on the compass but blows home a ship in which he is an owner.

RICHARD STEELE
The Spectator, 1711–1712

44

SIR ROGER AT CHURCH

MY friend Sir Roger, being a good churchman, has beautified the inside of his church with several texts of his own choosing: he has likewise given a handsome pulpit-cloth, and railed in the communion-table at his own expense. He has often told me that at his coming to his estate he found the parishioners very irregular; and that in order to make them kneel and join in the responses, he gave every one of them a hassock and a Common Prayer Book; and at the same time employed an itinerant singing-master, who goes about the country for that purpose, to instruct them rightly in the tunes of the psalms; upon which they now very much value themselves, and indeed outdo most of the country churches that I have ever heard.

As Sir Roger is landlord to the whole congregation, he keeps them in very good order, and will suffer nobody to sleep in it besides himself; for if by chance he has been surprised into a short nap at sermon, upon recovering out of it he stands up and looks about him, and if he sees anybody else nodding, either wakes them himself, or sends his servants to them. Several other of the old knight's peculiarities break out upon these occasions: sometimes he will be lengthening out a verse in the singing-psalms, half a minute after the rest of the congregation have done with it; sometimes, when he is pleased with the matter of his devotion, he pronounces Amen three or four times to the same prayer; and sometimes stands up when everybody else is upon their knees, to count the congregation, or see if any of his tenants are missing.

I was yesterday very much surprised to hear my old friend, in the midst of the service, calling out to one John Matthews to mind what he was about, and not disturb the congregation. This John Matthews it seems is remarkable for being an idle fellow, and at that time was kicking his heels for his diversion. This authority of the knight, though exerted in that odd manner which accompanies him in all circumstances of life, has a very good effect upon the parish, who are not polite enough to see anything ridiculous in his behaviour; besides that, the general good sense and worthiness of his character, make his friends observe these little singularities as foils that rather set off than blemish his good qualities.

As soon as the sermon is finished, nobody presumes to stir till Sir Roger is gone out of the church. The knight walks down from his seat in the chancel between a double row of his tenants, that stand bowing to him on each side; and every now and then enquires how such a one's wife, or mother, or son, or father do whom he does not see at church; which is understood as a secret reprimand to the person that is absent.

JOSEPH ADDISON
The De Coverley Papers, 1711-1712

45

PARSON TRULLIBER

PARSON Adams came to the house of Parson Trulliber, whom he found stripped into his waistcoat, with an apron on, and a pail in his hand, just come from serving his hogs; for Mr. Trulliber was a parson on Sundays, but all the other six might more properly be called a farmer. He occupied a small piece of land of his own, besides which he rented a considerable deal more. His wife milked his cows, managed his dairy, and followed the markets with butter and eggs. The hogs fell chiefly to his care, which he carefully waited on at home, and attended to fairs; on which occasion he was liable to make jokes, his own size being with much ale rendered little inferior to that of the beasts he sold. He was indeed one of the largest men you should see, and could have acted the part of Sir John Falstaff without stuffing. Add to this, that the rotundity of his belly was considerable increased by the shortness of his stature, his shadow ascending very near as far in height when he lay on his back, as when he stood on his legs. His voice was loud and hoarse, and his accents extremely broad; to complete the whole, he had a stateliness in his gait, when he walked, not unlike that of a goose, only he stalked slower.

HENRY FIELDING
Joseph Andrews, 1742

46

CORTEZ

THE history of the conquest of Mexico is necessarily that of Hernando Cortez, who is, if I may so, not merely the soul, but the body of the enterprise, present everywhere in person, in the thick of the fight or in the building of the works, with his sword or with his musket, sometimes leading his soldiers, and sometimes directing his little navy. The negotiations, intrigues, correspondence, are all conducted by him; and, like Caesar, he wrote his own Commentaries in the heat of the stirring scenes which form the subject of them. His character is marked with the most opposite traits, embracing qualities apparently the most incompatible. He was avaricious yet liberal; bold to desperation, yet cautious and calculating in his plans; magnanimous, yet very cunning; courteous and affable in his mien, yet inexorably stern; lax in his notions of morality, yet a sad bigot. The great feature in his character was constancy of purpose; a constancy not to be daunted by danger, nor baffled by disappointment, nor wearied out by impediments and delays. He was a knight-errant in the literal sense of the word. Of all the band of adventurous cavaliers whom Spain, in the sixteenth century, sent forth on the career of discovery and conquest, there was none more deeply filled with the spirit of romantic enterprise than Hernando Cortez. Dangers and difficulties instead of deterring seemed to have a charm in his eyes. They were necessary to arouse him to a full consciousness of his powers. He grappled with them at the outset, and, if I may so express myself, seemed to prefer to take his enterprises by the most difficult side. He conceived at the first moment of his landing in Mexico the design of its conquest. When he saw the strength of its civilisation, he was not turned from his purpose. When he was assailed by the superior force of Narvaez, he still persisted in it; and when he was driven in ruin from the capital, he still cherished his original idea. How successfully he carried it into execution we have seen.

W. H. PRESCOTT
The Conquest of Mexico, 1843

47

THE DUKE OF MEDINA SIDONIA

THE Duke of Medina Sidonia, named *El Bueno*, or the Good, was a grandee of highest rank. He was enormously rich, fond of hunting and shooting, a tolerable rider, for the rest a harmless creature getting on to forty, conscious of his defects, but not aware that so great a prince had any need to mend them; without vanity, without ambition, and most happy when lounging in his orange gardens at San Lucan. Of active service he had seen none. He was Captain-General of Andalusia, and had run away from Cadiz when Drake came into the harbour; but that was all. To his astonishment and his dismay he learnt that it was on him that the choice had fallen to be the Lord High Admiral of Spain and commander of the so much talked-of expedition to England. He protested his unfitness. He said he was no seaman; that he knew nothing of fighting by sea or land; that if he ventured out in a boat he was always sick; that he had never seen the English Channel; and that, as to politics, he neither knew nor cared anything about them. In short, he had not one qualification which such a post required.

JAMES ANTHONY FROUDE
English Seamen in the XVIth Century (lectures, 1893-4)

48

A JAILER

MY jailer's name was Ives. I was told he was a very self-willed person, not the more accomodating for being in a bad state of health; and that he called everybody *Mister*. "In short," said one of the tipstaves, "he is one as may be led, but he'll never be *druv*."

The sight of the prison-gate and the high wall was a dreary business. I thought of my horseback and the downs of Brighton; but congratulated myself, at all events, that I had come hither with a good conscience. After waiting in the prison-yard as long as if it had been the ante-room of a minister, I was at length ushered into the presence of the great man. He was in his parlour, which was decently furnished, and had a basin of broth before him, which he quitted on my appearance, and rose with much solemnity to meet me. He seemed about fifty years of age; had a white night-cap on, as if he was going to be hung, and a great red face, which looked ready to burst with blood. Indeed, he was not allowed by his physician to speak in a tone above a whisper. The first thing he said was, "Mister, I'd ha' given a matter of a hundred pounds, that you had not come to this place—a hundred pounds!" The emphasis which he had laid on the word "hundred" was enormous.

I forget what I said. I endeavoured, as usual, to make the best of things; but he recurred over and over again to the hundred pounds; and said he wondered, for his part, what the Government meant by sending me there, for the prison was not a prison fit for a gentleman. He often repeated this opinion afterwards, adding, with a peculiar nod of his head, "And, Mister, they knows it."

I said, that if a gentleman deserved to be sent to prison, he ought not to be treated with a greater nicety than anyone else: upon which he corrected me, observing very properly (though, as the phrase is, it was one word for the gentleman and two for his own apartments), that a person who had been used to a better mode of living than "low people" was not treated with the same justice, if forced to lodge exactly as they did. I told him his observation was very true; which gave him a favourable opinion of my understanding; for I had many occasions of remarking, that abstractedly considered he looked upon nobody whomsoever as his superior, speaking even of members of the royal family as persons whom he knew very well, and whom he estimated at no higher rate than became him. One Royal Duke had lunched in his parlour, and another he had laid under some polite obligation. "They knows me," said he, "very well, Mister; and, Mister, I knows them." This concluding sentence he uttered with great particularity and precision.

He was not proof, however, against a Greek Pindar, which he

happened to light upon one day among my books. Its unintelligible character gave him a notion that he had got somebody to deal with, who might really know something which he did not. Perhaps the gilt leaves and red morocco binding had their share in the magic. The upshot was, that he always showed himself anxious to appear well with me, as a clever fellow, treating me with great civilty on all occasions but one, when I made him very angry by disappointing him in a money amount. The Pindar was a mystery that staggered him. I remember very well, that giving me a long account one day of something connected with his business, he happened to catch with his eye the shelf that contained it, and whether he saw it or not, abruptly finished by observing, "But, Mister, you knows all these things as well as I do."

Upon the whole, my new acqaintance was as strange a person as I ever met with. A total want of education, together with a certain vulgar acuteness, conspired to render him insolent and pedantic. Disease sharpened his tendency to violent fits of passion, which threatened to suffocate him; and then in his intervals of better health he would issue forth, with his cock-up nose and his hat on one side, as great a fop as a jockey. I remember his coming to my rooms, about the middle of my imprisonment, as if on purpose to insult over my ill health with the contrast of his own convalescence, putting his arms in a gay manner a-kimbo, and telling me I should never live to go out, whereas he was riding about as stout as ever, and had just been in the country. He died before I left prison.

LEIGH HUNT

Essay on *My Jailers*)

49

THE PRISON GOVERNOR

We arrived at the prison, which stands in a narrow street not far from the great square. We entered a dusky passage at the end of which was a wicket door. My conductors knocked, a fierce visage peered through the wicket; there was an exchange of words, and in a few moments I found myself within the prison of Madrid, in a kind of corridor which overlooked at a considerable altitude what appeared to be a court, from which arose a hubbub of voices, and occasionally wild shouts and cries. Within the corridor, which served as a kind of office, were several people; one of them sat behind a desk, and to him the *alguazils*[1] went up, and after discoursing with him some time in low tones, delivered the warrant into his hands. He perused it with attention, then rising he advanced to me. What a figure! He was about forty years of age, and his height might have amounted to some six feet two inches, had he not been curved much after the fashion of the letter S. No weasel ever appeared lanker, and he looked as if a breath of air would have been sufficient to blow him away. His face might certainly have been called handsome, had it not been for its extraordinary and portentous meagreness; his nose was like an eagle's bill, his teeth white as ivory, his eyes black—oh, how black!—and fraught with a strange expression; his skin was dark, and the hair of his head like the plumage of the raven. A deep quiet smile dwelt continually on his features; but with all the quiet it was a cruel smile, such a one as would have graced the countenance of a Nero. "*Mais en revanche personne n'etoit plus honnête.*"[2] "*Caballero,*"[3] said he, "allow me to introduce myself to you as the *alcayde*[4] of this prison. I perceive by this paper that I am to have the honour of your company for a time, a short time doubtless, beneath this roof; I hope you will banish every apprehension from your mind. I am charged to treat you with all the respect which is due to the illustrious nation to which you belong, and which a cavalier of such exalted category as yourself is entitled to expect. A needless charge, it is true, as I should only have been too happy of my own accord to have afforded you every comfort and attention. *Caballero*, you will rather consider yourself here as a guest than as a prisoner; you will be permitted to roam over every part of this house whenever you think proper. You will find matters here not altogether below the attention of a

[1] constables. [2] But on the other hand nobody was more polished. [3] Your Honour! [4] Governor.

philosophic mind. Pray issue whatever commands you may think fit to the turnkeys and officials, even as if they were your own servants. I will now have the honour of conducting you to your apartment—the only one at present unoccupied. We invariably reserve it for cavaliers of distinction. I am happy to say that my orders are again in consonance with my inclination. No charge whatever will be made for it to you, though the daily hire of it is not unfrequently an ounce of gold. I entreat you, therefore, to follow me, cavalier, who am at all times and seasons the most obedient and devoted of your servants." Here he took off his hat and bowed profoundly.

Such was the speech of the *alcayde* of the prison of Madrid: a speech delivered in pure sonorous Castilian, with calmness, gravity, and almost with dignity; a speech which would have done honour to a a gentleman of high birth, to Monsieur Bassompierre, of the old Bastile, receiving an Italian prince, or the High Constable of the Tower an English duke attainted of high treason. Now, who in the name of wonder was this *alcayde*?

One of the greatest rascals in all Spain. A fellow who had more than once, by his grasping cupidity, and by his curtailment of the miserable rations of the prisoners, caused an insurrection in the court below, only to be repressed by bloodshed, and by summoning military aid; a fellow of low birth, who, only five years previous, had been *drummer* to a band of royalist volunteers!

But Spain is the land of extraordinary characters.

GEORGE BORROW

The Bible in Spain 1842

50

MRS. BATTLE

"A CLEAR fire, a clean hearth, and the rigour of the game." This was the celebrated *wish* of old Sarah Battle (now with God) who, next to her devotions, loved a good game of whist. She was none of your lukewarm gaemsters, your half and half players, who have no objection to take a hand, if you want one to make a rubber, who affirm that they have no pleasure in winning; that they like to win one game and lose another; that they can while away an hour very agreeably at a card-table, but are indifferent whether they play or no; and will desire an adversary, who has slipt a wrong card, to take it up and play another. These insufferable triflers are the curse of a table. One of these flies will spoil a whole pot. Of such it may be said, that they do not play at cards, but only play at playing them.

Sarah Battle was none of that breed. She detested them, as I do, from her heart and soul; and would not, save upon a striking emergency, willingly seat herself at the same table with them. She loved a thorough-paced partner, a determined enemy. She took, and gave, no concessions. She hated favours. She never made a revoke, nor passed it over in her adversary without exacting the utmost forfeiture. She fought a good fight; cut and thrust. She held not her good sword (her cards) "like a dancer." She sat bolt upright; and neither showed you her cards, nor desired to see yours. All people have their blind side—their superstitions; and I have heard her declare, under the rose, that Hearts was her favourite suit.

I never in my life—and I knew Sarah Battle many of the best years of it—saw her take out her snuff-box when it was her turn to play; or snuff a candle in the middle of a game; or ring for a servant, till it was fairly over. She never introduced or connived at, miscellaneous conversation during its process. As she emphatically observed, cards were cards; and if I ever saw unmingled distaste in her fine last-century countenance, it was at the airs of a young gentleman of a literary turn, who had been with difficulty persuaded to take a hand; and who, in his excess of candour, declared, that he thought there was no harm in unbending the mind now and then, after serious studies, in recreations of that kind! She could not bear to have her noble occupation, to which she wound up her faculties, considered in that light. It was her business, her duty, the thing she came into the world to do,—and she did it. She unbent her mind afterwards—over a book.

CHARLES LAMB
Essays of Elia, 1821

51

MR. AND MRS. BENNET

It is a truth universally acknowledged, that a single man in possession of a good fortune must be in want of a wife.

How ever little known the feelings or views of such a man may be on his first entering a neighbourhood, this truth is so well fixed in the minds of the surrounding families, that he is considered as the rightful property of some one or other of their daughters.

"My dear Mr. Bennet," said his lady to him one day, "have you heard that Netherfield Park is let at last?"

Mr. Bennet replied that he had not.

"But it is," returned she; "for Mrs. Long has just been here, and she told me all about it."

Mr. Bennet made no answer.

"Do you not want to know who has taken it?" cried his wife impatiently.

"*You* want to tell me, and I have no objection to hearing it."

This was invitation enough.

"Why, my dear, you must know, Mrs. Long says that Netherfield is taken by a young man of large fortune from the north of England; that he came down on Monday in a chaise and four to see the place, and was so much delighted with it, that he agreed with Mr. Morris immediately; that he is to take possession before Michaelmas, and some of his servants are to be in the house by the end of next week."

"What is his name?"

"Bingley."

"Is he married or single?"

"Oh! single, my dear, to be sure! A single man of large fortune; four or five thousand a year. What a fine thing for our girls!"

"How so? How can it affect them?"

"My dear Mr. Bennet," replied his wife, "how can you be so

tiresome! You must know that I am thinking of his marrying one of them."

"Is that his design in settling here?"

"Design! nonsense, how can you talk so! But it is very likely that he *may* fall in love with one of them, and therefore you must visit him as soon as he comes."

"I see no occasion for that. You and the girls may go, or you may send them by themselves, which perhaps will be still better, for as you are as handsome as any of them, Mr. Bingley might like you the best of the party."

"My dear, you flatter me. I certainly *have* had my share of beauty, but I do not pretend to be anything extraordinary now. When a woman has five grown-up daughters, she ought to give over thinking of her own beauty."

"In such cases, a woman has not often much beauty to think of."

"But, my dear, you must indeed go to see Mr. Bingley when he comes into the neighbourhood."

"It is more than I engage for, I assure you."

"But consider your daughters. Only think what an establishment it would be for one of them. Sir William and Lady Lucas are determined to go, merely on that account, for in general, you know, they visit no newcomers. Indeed you must go, for it will be impossible for *us* to visit him if you do not."

"You are over-scrupulous, surely. I dare say Mr. Bingley will be very glad to see you; and I will send a few lines by you to assure him of my hearty consent to his marrying whichever he chooses of the girls: though I must throw in a good word for my little Lizzy."

"I desire you will do no such thing. Lizzy is not a bit better than the others; and I am sure she is not half so handsome as Jane, nor half so good-humoured as Lydia. But you are always giving *her* the preference."

"They have none of them much to recommend them," replied he; "they are all silly and ignorant, like other girls; but Lizzy has something more of quickness than her sisters."

"Mr. Bennet, how can you abuse your own children in such a

way! You take delight in vexing me. You have no compassion on my poor nerves."

"You mistake me, my dear. I have a high respect for your nerves. They are my old friends. I have heard you mention them with consideration these twenty years at least."

"Ah! you do not know what I suffer."

"But I hope you will get over it, and live to see many young men of four thousand a year come into the neighbourhood."

"It will be no use to us, if twenty such should come, since you will not visit them."

"Depend upon it, my dear, that when there are twenty, I will visit them all."

Mr. Bennet was so odd a mixture of quick parts, sarcastic humour, reserve, and caprice, that the experience of three-and-twenty years had been insufficient to make his wife understand his character. *Her* mind was less difficult to develop. She was a woman of mean understanding, little information, and uncertain temper. When she was discontented, she fancied herself nervous. The business of her life was to get her daughters married; its solace was visiting and news.

JANE AUSTEN
Pride and Prejudice, 1797

52

SIR JOHN AND LADY MIDDLETON

In the evening, as Marianne was discovered to be musical, she was invited to play. The instrument was unlocked, everybody prepared to be charmed, and Marianne, who sang very well, at their request went through the chief of the songs which Lady Middleton had brought into the family on her marriage, and which had perhaps lain ever since in the same position on the pianoforte; for her ladyship had celebrated the event by giving up music, although by her mother's account she had played extremely well, and by her own was very fond of it.

Marianne's performance was highly applauded. Sir John was

loud in his admiration at the end of every song, and as loud in his conversation with the others while every song lasted. Lady Middleton frequently called him to order, wondered how any one's attention could be diverted from music for a moment, and asked Marianne to sing a particular song which Marianne had just finished.

JANE AUSTEN
Sense and Sensibility, 1811

53

SOCIETY AT BATH

GOING to the coffee-house one forenoon, I could not help contemplating the company, with equal surprise and compassion. We consisted of thirteen individuals: seven lamed by the gout, rheumatism, or palsy; three maimed by accident; and the rest either deaf or blind. One hobbled, another hopped, a third dragged his legs after him like a wounded snake, a fourth straddled between a pair of long crutches, like the mummy of a felon hanging in chains; a fifth was bent into a horizontal position, like a mounted telescope, shoved in by a couple of chairmen; and a sixth was the bust of a man, set upright in a wheel machine, which the waiter moved from place to place.

Being struck with some of their faces, I consulted the subscription-book; and, perceiving the names of several old friends, began to consider the group with more attention. At length I discovered Rear-Admiral Balderick, the companion of my youth, whom I had not seen since he was appointed lieutenant of the Severn. He was metamorphosed into an old man, with a wooden leg and a weather-beaten face; which appeared the more ancient from his grey locks, that were truly venerable. Sitting down at the table, where he was reading a newspaper, I gazed at him for some minutes, with a mixture of pleasure and regret, which made my heart gush with tenderness; then, taking him by the hand, "Ah Sam," said I, "forty years ago I little thought—" I was too much moved to proceed. "An old friend, sure enough!"

cried he, squeezing my hand, and surveying me eagerly through his glasses; "I know the looming of the vessel, though she has been hard strained since we parted; but I can't heave up the name." The moment I told him who I was, he exclaimed, "Ha! Matt, my old fellow-cruiser, still afloat!" and starting up, hugged me in his arms. His transport, however, boded me no good; for, in saluting me, he thrust the spring of his spectacles into my eye, and, at the same time, set his wooden stump upon my gouty toe; an attack that made me shed tears in sad earnest. After the hurry of our recognition was over, he pointed out two of our common friends in the room. The bust was what remained of Colonel Cockril, who had lost the use of his limbs in making an American campaign; and the telescope proved to be my college chum, Sir Reginald Bentley, who, with his new title and unexpected inheritance, commenced fox-hunter, without having served his apprenticeship in the mystery; and in consequence of following the hounds through a river, was seized with an inflammation in his bowels, which has contracted him into his present attitude.

TOBIAS SMOLLETT
Humphrey Clinker, 1771

54

BATHING MACHINES

THE Spa is a little way beyond the town[1], on this side, under a cliff, within a few paces of the sea, and thither the drinkers go every morning in deshabille; but the descent is by a great number of steps, which invalids find very inconvenient. Betwixt the well and the harbour, the bathing machines are ranged along the beach, with all their proper utensils and attendants. You have never seen one of these machines. Imagine to yourself a small, snug, wooden chamber, fixed upon a wheel-carriage, having a door at each end, and on each side a little window above, a bench below. The bather, ascending into his apartment by wooden steps, shuts himself in and begins to undress, while the attendant yokes

[1] Scarborough.

a horse to the end next the sea, and draws the carriage forwards till the surface of the water is on a level with the floor of the dressing-room, then he moves and fixes the horse to the other end. The person within, being stripped, opens the door to the seaward, where he finds the guide ready, and plunges headlong into the water. After having bathed, he re-ascends into the compartment by the steps, which had been shifted for that purpose, and puts on his clothes at his leisure, while the carriage is drawn back again upon the dry land; so that he has nothing further to do but to open the door, and come down as he went up. Should he be so weak or ill as to require a servant to put off and on his clothes, there is room enough in the apartment for half a dozen people. The guides who attend the ladies in the water are of their own sex; and they and the female bathers have a dress of flannel for the sea; nay, they are provided with other conveniences for the support of decorum. A certain number of the machines are fitted with tilts, that project from the seaward ends of them, so as to screen the bathers from the view of all persons whatsoever. The beach is admirably adapted for this purpose, the descent being very gradual, and the sand soft as velvet; but then the machines can be used only at a certain time of the tide, which varies every day; so that sometimes the bathers are obliged to rise very early in the morning.

TOBIAS SMOLLETT
Humphrey Clinker, 1771

55

A CRY OF FIRE

ON Saturday night, at eleven o'clock, when I had not been in bed five minutes, I was alarmed by a cry of fire, announced by two or three shrill screams upon our staircase. Our servants, who were going to bed, saw it from their windows, and in appearance so near, that they thought our house in danger. I immediately rose, and putting by the curtain, saw sheets of fire rising above the ridge of Mr. Palmer's house, opposite to ours. The deception was such, that I had no doubt it had begun with *him*, but soon found that it was rather farther off. In fact, it was at three places;—in the outhouses belonging to George Griggs, Lucy and Abigail Tyrrel. Having broke out in three different parts, it is supposed to have been maliciously kindled. A tar-barrel and a quantity of tallow made a most tremendous blaze, and the buildings it had seized upon being all thatched, the appearance became every moment more formidable. Providentially, the night was perfectly calm; so calm that candles without lanterns, of which there were multitudes in the street, burnt steadily as in a house. By four in the morning it was so far reduced, that all danger seemed to be over; but the confusion it had occasioned was almost infinite. Every man who supposed his dwelling-house in jeopardy, emptied it as fast as he could, and conveyed his movables to the house of some neighbour, supposed to be more secure. Ours, in the space of two hours, was so filled with all sorts of lumber, that we had not even room for a chair by the fireside. George Griggs is the principal sufferer. He gave eighteen guineas, or nearly that sum, to a woman whom, in his hurry, he mistook for his wife; but the supposed wife walked off with the money, and he will probably never recover it. He has likewise lost forty pounds' worth of wool. London never exhibited a scene of greater depredation, drunkenness, and riot. Everything was stolen that could be got at, and every drop of liquor drunk that was not guarded. Only one thief has yet been detected; a woman of the name of J———, who was stopped by young Handscomb with an apron full of plunder. He was forced to strike her down, before he could wrest it from her. Could you visit the place, you would see a most striking proof of a Providence interposing to stop the progress of the flames. They had almost reached, that is to say, within six yards of Daniel Raban's wood-pile, in which were fifty pounds' worth of faggots and furze; and exactly there they were extinguished; otherwise, especially if a breath of air had happened to move, all that side of the town must probably have been consumed. After all this dreadful conflagration, we find nothing burnt but the outhouses; and the dwellings to which they belonged have suffered only the damage of being unroofed on that side next the fire. No lives were lost, nor any limbs broken.

WILLIAM COWPER
Letter, 1783

56

A CAIRO DRUGGIST

HIS little shop in the Jemeliyyah Quarter is a perfect gem of Nilotic queerness. A hole about five feet long and six deep, pierced in the wall of some house, it is divided into two compartments, separated by a thin partition of wood, and communicating by a kind of arch cut in the boards. The inner box, germ of a back parlour, acts as a storeroom, as the pile of empty old baskets tossed in dusty confusion upon the dirty floor shows.

In front is displayed the stock in trade, a matting full of Persian tobacco and pipe-bowls of red clay, a palm-leaf bag, containing vile coffee and large lumps of coarse, whitey-brown sugar wrapped up in brown paper. On the shelves and ledges are rows of well-thumbed wooden boxes, labelled with the greatest carelessness, pepper for rhubarb, arsenic for Tafl, or wash-clay, and sulphate of iron where sal-ammoniac should be.

There is also a square case containing, under lock and key, small change and some choice articles of commerce, damaged perfumes, bad antimony for the eyes, and pernicious rouge. And dangling close above it is a rusty pair of scales, ill poised enough for Egyptian Themis herself to use.

To hooks over the shop front are suspended reeds for pipes, tallow candles, dirty wax tapers and cigarette paper: instead of plate-glass windows and brass-handled doors, a ragged net keeps away the flies when the master is in, and the thieves when he goes out to recite in the Hasanyn mosque his daily chapter, "Ya Sin". A wooden shutter which closes down at night-time, and by day two palm-stick stools intensely dirty and full of fleas, occupying the place of the Mastabah or earthern bench, which accommodated purchasers, complete the furniture of my preceptor's[1] establishment.

There he sits, or rather lies (for verily I believe he sleeps through three-fourths of the day), a thin old man, about fifty-eight, with features once handsome and regular; a sallow face, shaven head, deeply wrinkled cheeks, eyes hopelessly bleared, and a rough grey beard ignorant of oil and comb. His turban, though large, is brown with wear; his coat and small-clothes display many a hole; and though his face and hands must be frequently washed preparatory to devotion, still they have the quality of looking always unclean.

It is wonderful how fierce and gruff he is to the little boys and girls who flock to him grasping farthings for pepper and sugar. On such occasions I sit admiring to see him, when forced to exertion, wheel about on his place, making a pivot of that portion of our organisation which mainly distinguishes our species from the other families of the Simiadae, to reach some distant drawer, or pull down a case from its accustomed shelf. How does he manage to say his prayers, to kneel and to prostrate himself upon that two feet of ragged rug, scarcely sufficient for a British infant to lie upon? He hopelessly owns that he knows nothing of his craft, and the seats before his shop are seldom occupied.

SIR RICHARD BURTON
A Pilgrimage to Mecca, 1855

57

ARRIVAL OF A CARAVAN

I AROSE in the morning, and looked out from the window of the Majlis.[2] The Barr-el-Manakhah,[3] from a dusty waste dotted with a few Bedawi hair-tents, had assumed all the various shapes and the colours of a kaleidoscope. The eye was bewildered by the shifting of innumerable details, in all parts totally different

[1] preceptor: teacher. The druggist had agreed to give the author lessons in Arabic. [2] Majlis: parlour (of the house where he was staying). [3] Barr-el-Manakhah: An open space on the outskirts of Medina, where the great Caravan from Damascus, here described, assembled with smaller caravans on their way to Meccah.

from one another, thrown confusedly together in one small field; and, however jaded with sight-seeing, it dwelt with delight upon the variety, the vivacity, and the intense picturesqueness of the scene. In one night had sprung up a town of tents of every size, colour, and shape; round, square, and oblong; open and closed—from the shawl-lined and gilt-topped pavilion of the Pasha, with all the luxurious appurtenances of the Haram, to its neighbour the little dirty green "rowtie" of the tobacco-seller. They were pitched in admirable order here ranged in a long line, where a street was required: there packed in dense masses, where thoroughfares were unnecessary.

But how describe the utter confusion in the crowding, the bustling, and the vast variety and volume of sound? Huge white Syrian dromedaries, compared with which those of El-Hejaz appeared mere pony-camels; jingling large bells, and bearing Shugdufs (litters) like miniature green tents, swaying and tossing upon their backs; gorgeous Takhtrawan, or litters carried between camels or mules with scarlet and brass trappings; Bedawin bestriding naked-backed "Daluls" (dromedaries), and clinging like apes to the hairy humps; Arnaut, Kurd, and Turkish irregular cavalry, fiercer looking in their mirth than Roman peasants in their rage; fainting Persian pilgrims, forcing their stubborn camels to kneel, or dismounted grumbling from jaded donkeys; Kahwajis, sherbet sellers, and ambulant tobacconists crying their goods; countrypeople driving flocks of sheep and goats with infinite clamour through lines of horses fiercely snorting and biting and kicking and rearing; townspeople seeking their friends; returned travellers exchanging affectionate salutes; devout Hajis[1] jostling one another, running under the legs of camels, and tumbling over the tents' ropes in their hurry to reach the Haram; cannon roaring from the citadel; shopmen, water-carriers, and fruit vendors fighting over their bargains; boys bullying heretics with loud screams; a well-mounted party of fine old Arab Shaykhs of the Hamidah clan, preceded by their varlets, performing the Arzah or war dance—compared with which the Pyrenean bear's performance is grace itself—firing their duck-

[1] Haji: pilgrim.

guns upwards, or blowing the powder into the claves of those before them, brandishing their swords, leaping frantically the while, with their bright-coloured rags floating in the wind, tossing their long spears tufted with ostrich feathers high in the air, reckless where they fall; servants seeking their masters, and masters their tents, with vain cries of Ya Mohammed;[1] grandees riding mules or stalking on foot, preceded by their crowd-beaters, shouting to clear the way; here the loud shrieks of women and children, whose litters are bumping and rasping against one another; there the low moaning of some poor wretch that is seeking a shady corner to die in: and a thick dust which blurs the outlines like a London fog, with a flaming sun that draws sparkles of fire from the burnished weapons of the crowd, and the brass balls of tents and litter; and—I doubt, gentle reader, that even the length, the jar, and the confusion of this description is adequate to its subject, or that any "word-painting" of mine can convey a just idea of the scene.

SIR RICHARD BURTON

A Pilgrimage to Mecca 1855

58

A WRESTLING MATCH IN TAHITI

WHEN all was ready, ten or twelve persons, whom we understood to be the combatants, and who were naked, except a cloth that was fastened about the waist, entered the area, and walked slowly round it, in a stooping posture, with their left hands upon their right breasts, and their right hands open, with which they struck the left forearm so as to produce a quick smart sound. This was a general challenge to the combatants whom they were to engage, or to any other person present. After these followed others in the same manner; and then a particular challenge was given, by which each man singled out his antagonist: this was done by joining the finger-ends of both hands, and bringing them to the breast, at the same time moving the elbows up and down with a quick motion. If the person to whom this was addressed

[1] One might as sensibly cry out 'John' in an English theatre.

accepted the challenge, he repeated the signs, and immediately each put himself into an attitude to engage; the next minute they closed; but, except in first seizing each other, it was a mere contest of strength. Each endeavoured to lay hold of the other, first by the thigh, and, if that failed, by the hand, the hair, the cloth, or elsewhere as he could. When this was done, they grappled, without the least dexterity or skill, till one of them, by having a more advantageous hold, or greater muscular force, threw the other on his back. When the contest was over, the old men gave their plaudits to the victor in a few words, which they repeated together in a kind of tune: his conquest was also generally celebrated by three huzzas. The entertainment was then suspended for a few minutes; after which another couple of wrestlers came forward and engaged in the same manner. If it happened that neither was thrown, after the contest had continued about a minute, they parted, either by consent or the intervention of their friends; and in this case each slapped his arm, as a challenge to a new engagement either with the same antagonist or some other. While the wrestlers were engaged, another party of men performed a dance, which lasted also about a minute; but neither of these parties took the least notice of each other, their attention being wholly fixed on what they were doing. We observed with pleasure that the conqueror never exulted over the vanquished, and that the vanquished never repined at the success of the conqueror: the whole contest was carried on with perfect good-will and good-humour, though in the presence of at least five hundred spectators.

JAMES COOK
Journals, 1769

59

DRY-FLY FISHING

THE angler is by the river not later than ten o'clock: the stream is lively but quiet, and here and there the surface is broken by the recurring swirl of a swaying weed; but no life disturbs it, except the occasional dive of a dab-chick, the movements of a watcher or water-vole. Not a bird skims the surface of the water, not a fly is to be seen on it, not a sign of living creature under it. But the fresh light air is like a caress, the warm sun shines interrupted only by the occasional passage of small white clouds, the water meadows are bright with buttercups, and the woods and hedges that are on their borders are white with hawthorn blossom or lit by the candelabra of horse-chestnut flower. Birds of many sorts, most notably blackbirds, are singing, and the angler in his hour of waiting has such entertainment as seems more than imperfect man can deserve or comprehend. Presently—it may be soon or not till after an hour or more—flies begin to appear on the surface of the water, the rise of a trout is seen: in a short time all is life and agitation. Trout are rising everywhere, some audibly, some without sound; flies are hatching out all over the river, sitting or skipping in little flights on the water or rising into the air; a moving network of birds, swifts, swallows, and martins, is on the river; a rush of bird life and the swish of the wings of the swifts is heard as they pass and repass up and down the stream; and the angler, no longer inert, is on his knees in the midst of it all, at convenient distance from a rising trout, one arm in constant action and the rod and line making a busy sound in the air as he dries and casts his fly. Now for two hours or more his life is energy, expectation, anxiety, resource, and effort. After two hours or so the rise begins to slacken; in time it becomes difficult to find a rising fish, and the fish when found is fastidious and hard to tempt; and by two or three or four o'clock, as the case may be, the river has become as lifeless as when the angler first stood by the bank in the morning. The water glides, fresh as ever; the weeds wave, but the rise of fly and fish is over and swifts and swallows and martins have withdrawn to the upper air, or to their various abodes.

VISCOUNT GREY
Fallodon Papers, 1926

60

FIVE OF THE CLOCK

IT is now five of the clock, and the sun is going apace upon his journey; and fie sluggards who would be asleep: the bells ring to prayer, and the streets are full of people, and the highways are stored with travellers: the scholars are up and going to school, and the rods are ready for the truants' correction: the maids are at milking, and the servants at plough, and the wheel goes merrily, while the mistress is by: the capons and the chickens must be served without door, and the hogs cry till they have their swill; the shepherd is almost gotten to his fold, and the herd begins to blow his horn through the town. The blind fiddler is up with his dance and his song, and the alehouse door is unlocked for good fellows: the hounds begin to find after the hare, and horse and foot follow after the cry: the traveller now is well on his way, and if the weather be fair, he walks with the better cheer: the carter merrily whistles to his horse, and the boy with his sling casts stones at the crows: the lawyer now begins to look on his case, and if he give good counsel, he is worthy of his fee. In brief, not to stay too long upon it, I hold it the necessity of labour, and the note of profit.

NICHOLAS BRETON

The Fantasticks, 1626

(3) *INDUSTRY AND DISCOVERY*

61

HARVESTING IN SCOTLAND

TRAVELLING in the north part of Britain, I observed, that in the time of their harvest, they had always an overseer to keep the reapers to their work, and a bag-pipe to encourage them while they were at work: and one of our company observing that we had no such merry doings at our harvests in England; another answered him, 'twas true, nor was there any need of it, for that the English worked merrily enough without music; adding, our workmen have good victuals and good drink: Let's enquire how these poor people feed, said he; and so we did, when we found that the best of their provision was a cake of oat bread, which they call a bannock, and a draught of water only; and twice in the day, the farmer or steward gave them every one a dram of Glasgow brandy, as they called it; that is to say, good malt spirits.

Upon the whole, it was evident, the poor men had need enough of music to encourage them at their labour; nor would the music do neither, without the overseer or steward being in the field too, to see that they stood to their work.

In England we see the farmers in harvest time, providing good beef and mutton, pies, puddings, and other provisions to a strange profusion, feasting their workmen rather than feeding them; and giving them good wages besides: But let any man see the difference of the work, these need no music, the feast is better than the fiddle, and the pudding does more than the bag-pipe: in short, they work with a vigour and spirit, not to be seen in other countries.

DANIEL DEFOE

A Plan of the English Commerce, 1728

62

FELLING TREES

WE had nearly threaded the wood, and were approaching an open grove of magnificent oaks on the other side, when sounds other than of nightingales burst on our ear, the deep and frequent strokes of the woodman's axe, and emerging from the Pinge we discovered the havoc which that axe had committed. Above twenty of the finest trees lay stretched on the velvet turf. There they lay in every shape and form of devastation: some, bare trunks stripped ready for the timber carriage, with the bark built up in long piles at the side; some with the spoilers busy about them, stripping, hacking, hewing; others with their noble branches, their brown and fragrant shoots all fresh as if they were alive—majestic corpses, the slain of to-day! The grove was like a field of battle. The young lads who were stripping the bark, the very children who were picking up the chips, seemed awed and silent, as if conscious that death was around them. The nightingales sang faintly and interruptedly—a few low frightened notes like a requiem.

Ah! here we are at the very scene of murder, the very tree that they are felling; they have just hewn round the trunk with those slaughtering axes, and are about to saw it asunder. After all, it is a fine and thrilling operation, as the work of death usually is. Into how grand an attitude was that young man thrown as he gave the final strokes round the root; and how wonderful is the effect of that supple and apparently powerless saw—bending like a riband, and yet overmastering that giant of the woods, conquering and overthrowing that thing of life! Now it has passed half through the trunk, and the woodman has begun to calculate which way the tree will fall; he drives a wedge to direct its course; —now a few more movements of the noiseless saw; and then a larger wedge. See how the branches tremble! Hark how the trunk begins to crack! Another stroke of the huge hammer on the wedge, and the tree quivers, as with a mortal agony, shakes, reels, and falls. How slow, and solemn, and awful it is! How like to death, to human death in its grandest form! Caesar in the Capitol, Seneca in the bath, could not fall more sublimely than that oak.

Even the heavens seem to sympathise with the devastation. The clouds have gathered into one thick low canopy, dark and vapoury as the smoke which overhangs London; the setting sun is just gleaming underneath with a dim and bloody glare, and the crimson rays spreading upward with a lurid and portentous grandeur, a subdued and dusky glow, like the light reflected on the sky from some vast conflagration. The deep flush fades away, and the rain begins to descend; and we hurry homeward rapidly, yet sadly, forgetful alike of the flowers, the hedgehog, and the wetting, thinking and talking only of the fallen tree.

MARY RUSSELL MITFORD
Our Village, 1824-32

63

HOP-PICKING (1)

HOPPING was the season for school-holidays in Farnham: a season of blowsy careless open-air life—not too comfortable, yet always enjoyable, with just a touch of excitement in it. It was shabby, jolly; it gave you an appetite. You wore old clothes and might go dirty; and on the whole it was golden and warm September weather—easy-going sunburnt autumn weather. To be sure, "Hopping mornings" was a phrase with special meaning in Farnham: it seemed to fit exactly the early hours, just after sunrise in September, while the air was chilly from the night and fingers ached, and a touch of frost made you wish for breakfast and something hot to drink. The really bad weather for hopping was steady rain, when pickers stayed away altogether, though hundreds would generally draggle into the hop-ground of a morning—say at about half-past six—in hopes that the weather would clear soon. As a rule however I remember hopping as a quiet and glowing time, warm, a little fatigued. September could even be too fine—too hot. In this case pickers would sometimes make a screen for themselves of poles already "picked", to shade their "standings" from too wearisome a spell of sunshine, when you stood hour after hour, picking hops into a basket.

And, even with that screen, hot sun could be really harmful. A properly ripe hop, fit to pick, was firm and stiff between the fingers and heavy with yellow-golden dust—and helped to fill the basket: but in hot weather the hops were limp—"wilty" as we said—and did not soon enough make up a bushel.

And it was by the bushel that the picking of hops was paid for. Pickers who were out to earn money—and many Farnham folk took their annual holiday that way—would "take a frame", that is to say engage themselves to an owner of hops, to be responsible for picking into one of his seven-bushel baskets until the crop was harvested. Up the sides of the big long baskets black marks measured the bushels; and if the hops were "wilty" it took too long to reach and pass one of these marks, and the pickers felt tired and stifled and cross. At such times a little boy could get plenty of testy words and sour looks by blundering carelessly against a basket. The contents would too easily shake down to show a smaller measure. When the basket was full enough,—at least you hoped it might be full enough,—you could make it look a little fuller still by plunging both arms in deep and "lightening" the hops in it. Then you called out "Tallyman"—and the grower's representative came with his book (no longer tallies, in my time) to enter what you had picked. He was likely to scrutinise the basket rather carefully, lest there should be too many leaves in it. A certain sort of pickers, out to make money and working too fast, probably needed looking after. "Scratchers" they were called by other pickers. The full basket was emptied into a "sarplice"—a wide open bag of coarse brown sacking, skewered over a wooden "frame" and hung conveniently near to a "setting" of pickers. The sarplice (sarplier was its more correct name—but we lived near Farnham Castle, and may have thought "sarplice" would sound better to the Bishop) would hold eighteen bushels or so and then could be skewered up and swung into a cart and taken to the kiln for drying.

64

HOP-PICKING (2)

It was a pleasant thing in the dusky autumn evenings to pass close in Farnham streets to a load of freshly picked hops. There were many such loads, and most fragrant they were! The very streets smelt of hops as the cart went lumbering along and every load of bulging sarplices told to a native of the town what had been going on all round him. Truly to think now of the loaded waggons and carts is to recover weeks of strong rough open-air autumn. Those plump earth-coloured, yet greenish, sacks, lying a-tumble all across the cart, meant so much. To see them was to see, and smell, the picturesque dismantling of a hop-ground—to hear the day-long chatter as of a flock of depredating birds; to catch the frequent laugh, the garrulous squabble, the rustle of the bines, the squalling of children. "Tallyman" has been mentioned; oftener still sounded the cry "Pole-puller"—for every ground had one or two men (I remember one went by the name of "Ginger") whose duty was to keep the pickers supplied with "poles", while of course he was responsible to the grower for due care of the plant. With a strong pocket-knife he cut all the bines of a pole twelve inches or so above the soil; with an ingenious implement called a Hop-dog he lifted the leaf-covered poles out of the ground; and so he laid them down beside the "frame" they had been allotted to, ready for the pickers to pick up and place over the basket for themselves, as soon as they were ready to gather the crop. (By the way, though the hops grew in bunches, and often a big bunch was torn whole from the bine, the hops had to be separated from it and put into the basket one by one.) I do not remember pole-pullers as individual men; but a memory of showy colour comes to me, soon resolved into sun-tanned skin, hairs shining curly on strong arms, hop-growth and sky; and, on the ground, a pile of men's things—white "slops", yellow straw baskets, a black leather strap or so, a glass bottle with tea showing through it, a dark brown wooden beer-bottle shaped like a tiny barrel. Corduroy trousers and red cotton handkerchiefs add to the gaudy colour effect.

All day long the picking goes on; women scold at their children, who will neither work nor be still. "Let me catch you, you young ninter, I'll gie you the bine!" (the bine being hop bine, tough and twisty, like thin rope—a handy whip). So, for hours, the pickers stand—scolding, laughing, chattering, calling; until at last, between five and six o'clock, the cry goes across the ground "No more poles!" For in fact enough hops have now been got to keep the kilns going until morning. So, as the poles already "pulled" are finished, the tallyman makes his last round for the day, the sarplices are skewered up and carried to the cart (this is the pole-puller's job, horses in fact being too heavy to travel promiscuously over soil that must always be kept light) and meanwhile the fagged pickers gather together their things and straggle away in little groups or in families.

GEORGE STURT
A Small Boy in the Sixties, 1927

65

COOKING IN AFRICA

In preparing their corn for food, the natives use a large wooden mortar called a *paloon*, in which they bruise the seed until it parts with the outer covering, or husk, which is then separated from the clean corn by exposing it to the wind; nearly in the same manner as wheat is cleared from the chaff in England. The corn thus freed from the husk is returned to the mortar, and beaten into meal, which is dressed variously in different countries; but the most common preparation of it among the nations of the Gambia, is a sort of pudding, which they call *kouskous*. It is made by first moistening the flour with water, and then stirring and shaking it about in a large calabash or gourd, till it adheres together in small granules, resembling sago. It is then put into an earthen pot, whose bottom is perforated with a number of small holes; and this pot being placed upon another, the two vessels are luted together, either with a paste of meal and water, or with cow's dung, and placed upon the fire. In the lower vessel is commonly some animal food and water, the steam or vapour of which ascends through the perforations in the bottom of the upper vessel, and softens and prepares the *kouskous*, which is very much esteemed throughout all the countries that I visited. I am informed that the same manner of preparing flour is very generally used on the Barbary Coast, and that the dish so prepared is there called by the same name. It is therefore probable that the Negroes borrowed the practice from the Moors.

MUNGO PARK
Travels in the Interior of Africa, 1799

66

MAIZE BREAD

In Central America, the bread made from the maize is prepared at the present day exactly as it was in ancient Mexico. The grain is first of all boiled along with wood ashes or a little lime; the alkali loosens the outer skin of the grain, and this is rubbed off with the hands in running water, a little of it at a time, placed upon a slightly concave stone, called a *metlate*, from the Aztec *metlatl*, on which it is rubbed with another stone shaped like a rolling-pin. A little water is thrown on it as it is bruised, and it is thus formed into paste. A ball of the paste is taken and flattened out between the hands into a cake about ten inches diameter and three-sixteenths of an inch thick, which is baked on a slightly concave earthenware pan. The cakes so made are called *tortillas*, and are very nutritious. When travelling, I preferred them myself to bread made from wheaten flour. When well made and eaten warm, they are very palatable.

THOMAS BELT
A Naturalist in Nicaragua, 1874

67

PATAGONIAN GAUCHOS

One evening a "domidor" (a subduer of horses) came for the purpose of breaking-in some colts. I will describe the preparatory steps, for I believe they have not been mentioned by other travellers. A troop of wild young horses is driven into the corral, or large enclosure of stakes, and the door is shut. We will suppose that one man alone has to catch and mount a horse which as yet had never felt bridle or saddle. I conceive, except by a Gaucho, such a feat would be utterly impracticable. The Gaucho picks out a full-grown colt; and as the beast rushes round the circus, he throws his lazo so as to catch both the front legs. Instantly the horse rolls over with a heavy shock, and whilst struggling on the ground, the Gaucho, holding the lazo tight, makes a circle, so as to catch one of the hind legs, just beneath the fetlock, and draws it close to the two front legs: he then hitches the lazo, so that the three are bound together. Then sitting on the horse's neck, he fixes a strong bridle, without a bit, to the lower jaw: this he does by passing a narrow thong through the eye-holes at the end of the reins, and several times round both jaw and tongue. The two front legs are now tied closely together with a strong leathern thong, fastened by a slip-knot. The lazo, which bound the three together, being then loosed, the horse rises with difficulty. The Gaucho now holding fast the bridle fixed to the lower jaw, leads the horse outside the corral. If a second man is present (otherwise the trouble is much greater) he holds the animal's head, whilst the first puts on the horsecloths and saddle, and girths the whole together. During this operation, the horse, from dread and astonishment at thus being bound round the waist, throws himself over and over again on the ground, and, till beaten, is unwilling to rise. At last, when the saddling is finished, the poor animal can hardly breathe from fear, and is white with foam and sweat. The man now prepares to mount by pressing heavily on the stirrup, so that the horse may not lose its balance; and at the moment that he throws his leg over the animal's back, he pulls the slip-knot binding the front legs, and the beast is free. Some "domidors" pull the knot while the animal is lying on the ground, and, standing over the saddle, allow him to rise beneath them. The horse, wild with dread, gives a few most violent bounds, and then starts off at full gallop: when quite exhausted, the man, by patience, brings him back to the corral, where, reeking hot and scarcely alive, the poor beast is let free. Those animals which will not gallop away, but obstinately throw themselves on the ground, are by far the most troublesome. This process is tremendously severe, but in two or three trials the horse is tamed. It is not, however, for some weeks that the animal is ridden with the iron bit and solid ring, for it must learn to associate the will of its rider with the feel of the rein, before the most powerful bridle can be of any service.

CHARLES DARWIN
The Voyage of the Beagle, 1839

68

BEAR-HUNTING IN LAPLAND

HUNTING and fishing are the principal employments of the Lapp tribes; and to slay a bear is the most honourable exploit a Lapp hero can achieve. The flesh of the slaughtered beast becomes the property, not of the man who killed him, but of him who discovered his trail; and the skin is hung up on a pole for the wives of all who took part in the expedition to shoot at with their eyes bandaged. Fortunate is she whose arrow pierces the trophy—not only does it become her prize, but in the eyes of the whole settlement her husband is looked upon thenceforth as the most fortunate of men. As long as the chase is going on, the women are not allowed to stir abroad; but as soon as the party have safely brought home their booty, the whole female population issues from the tents, and having deliberately chewed some bark of a species of alder, they spit the red juice into their husband's faces, typifying thereby the bear's blood which has been shed in the honourable encounter.

LORD DUFFERIN
Letters from High Latitudes, 1856-7

69

TRAVELLING IN THE DESERT

WE journeyed on till near sunset through the wilderness without *ennui*. It is strange how the mind can be amused by scenery that presents so few objects to occupy it. But in such a country every slight modification of form or colour rivets observation: the senses are sharpened, and the perceptive faculties, prone to sleep over a confused mass of natural objects, act vigorously when excited by the capability of embracing each detail. Moreover, Desert views are eminently suggestive; they appeal to the Future, not to the Past; they arouse because they are by no means memorial.

To the solitary wayfarer there is an interest in the Wilderness unknown to Cape seas and Alpine glaciers, and even to the rolling Prairie—the effect of continued excitement on the mind, stimulating its powers to their pitch. Above, through a sky terrible in its stainless beauty, and the splendours of a pitiless blinding glare, the Simum caresses you like a lion with flaming breath. Around lie drifted sand-heaps, upon which each puff of wind leaves its trace in solid waves, flayed rocks, the very skeletons of mountains, and hard unbroken plains, over which he who rides is spurred by the idea that the bursting of a water-skin, or the pricking of a camel's hoof, would be a certain death of torture; a haggard land infested with wild beasts, and wilder men; a region whose very fountains murmur the warning words "Drink and away!"

In the Desert, even more than upon the ocean, there is present death: hardship is there, and piracies, and shipwreck, solitary, not in crowds, where, as the Persians say, "Death is a Festival"; and this sense of danger, never absent, invests the scene of travel with an interest not its own.

Let the traveller, who suspects exaggeration, leave the Suez road for an hour or two, and gallop northwards over the sands: in the drear silence, the solitude, and the fantastic desolation of the place, he will feel what the Desert may be. And then the Oases, and little lines of fertility—how soft and how beautiful—even though the Wady el-Ward (the Vale of Flowers) be the name of some stern flat upon which a handful of wild shrubs blossom while struggling through a cold season's ephemeral existence.

In such circumstances the mind is influenced through the body. Though your mouth glows, and your skin is parched, yet you feel no languor, the effect of humid heat; your lungs are lightened, your sight brightens, your memory recovers its tone, and your spirits become exuberant; your fancy and imagination are powerfully aroused, and the wildness and sublimity of the scenes around you stir up all the energies of your soul—whether for exertion, danger, or strife. Your morale improves: you become frank and cordial, hospitable and single-minded: the hypocritical politeness and the slavery of civilisation are left behind you in the city. Your senses are quickened: they require no stimulants but air and exercise—in the Desert spirituous liquors excite only disgust.

There is a keen enjoyment in mere animal existence. The

sharp appetite disposes of the most indigestible food; the sand is softer than a bed of down, and the purity of the air suddenly puts to flight a dire cohort of diseases.

SIR RICHARD BURTON
A Pilgrimage to Mecca, 1855

70

KANO: A WEST AFRICAN CITY

THE city is of an irregular oval shape, about fifteen miles in circumference, and surrounded by a clay wall thirty feet high, with a dry ditch along the inside, and another on the outside. There are fifteen gates, including one lately built up. The gates are of wood, covered with sheet iron, and are regularly opened and shut at sunrise and sunset. A platform inside, with two guard-houses below it, serves to defend each entrance. Not more than one fourth of the ground within the walls is occupied by houses: the vacant space is laid out in fields and gardens. The large morass, nearly intersecting the city from east to west, and crossed by a small neck of land, on which the market is held, is overflowed in the rainy season. The water of the city being considered unwholesome, women are constantly employed hawking water about the streets, from the favourite springs in the neighbourhood. The houses are built of clay, and are mostly of a square form, in the Moorish fashion, with a central room, the roof of which is supported by the trunks of palm trees, where visitors and strangers are received. The apartments of the ground floor open into this hall of audience, and are generally used as store-rooms. A staircase leads to an open gallery overlooking the hall, and serving as a passage to the chambers of the second story, which are lighted with small windows. In the back courtyard there is a well and other conveniences. Within the enclosure in which the house stands, there are also a few round huts of clay, roofed with the stalks of Indian corn, and thatched with long grass. These are usually very neat and clean, and of a much larger size than those of Bornou. The governor's residence covers a large space, and resembles a walled village. It even contains a mosque, and several towers three or four stories high, with windows in the European style, but without glass or framework. It is necessary to pass through two of these towers in order to gain the suite of inner apartments occupied by the governor.

HUGH CLAPPERTON
Travels in Africa, 1826

71

THE MARKET AT KANO

THE soug, or market, is well supplied with every necessary and luxury in request among the people of the interior. It is held, as I have mentioned, on a neck of land between two swamps; and as this site is covered with water during the rainy season, the holding it here is consequently limited to the dry months, when it is numerously frequented as well by strangers as inhabitants: indeed, there is no market in Africa so well regulated. The sheikh of the soug lets the stalls at so much a month, and the rent forms a part of the revenues of the governor. The sheikh of the soug also fixes the prices of all wares, for which he is entitled to a small commission, at the rate of fifty whydah or cowries, on every sale amounting to four dollars or 8,000 cowries, according to the standard exchange between silver money and this shell currency. There is another custom regulated with equal certainty and in universal practice: the seller returns to the buyer a stated part of the price, by way of blessing, as they term it, or of lucky-penny, according to our less devout phraseology. This is a discount of two per cent. on the purchase money; but, if the bargain is made in a hired house, it is the landlord who receives the luck-penny. I may here notice the great convenience of the cowrie, which no forgery can imitate; and which, by the dexterity of the natives in reckoning the largest sums, forms a ready medium of exchange in all transactions from the lowest to the highest. Particular quarters are appropriated to distinct articles; the smaller wares being set out in booths in the middle, and cattle and bulky commodities being exposed to sale in the outskirts of the market-place: wood, dried grass, bean straw for provender, beans, Guinea corn, Indian corn, wheat, &c., are in one quarter; goats, sheep, asses, bullocks, horses, and camels, in another; earthenware and indigo in a third; vegetables and fruit of all descriptions, such as yams, sweet potatoes, water and musk melons, pappaw fruit, limes, cashew nuts, plums, mangoes, shaddocks, dates, &c., in a fourth, and so on. Wheaten flour is baked into bread of three different kinds; one like muffins, another like our twists, and the third a light puffy cake, with honey and melted butter poured over it. Rice is also made into little cakes. Beef and mutton are killed daily. Camel flesh is occasionally to be had, but is often meagre; the animal being commonly killed, as an Irish grazier might say, to save its life: it is esteemed a great delicacy, however, by the Arabs, when the carcass is fat. The native butchers are fully as knowing as our own, for they make a few slashes to show the fat, blow up meat, and sometimes even stick a little sheep's wool on a leg of goat's flesh, to make it pass with the ignorant for mutton. When a fat bull is brought to market to be killed, its horns are dyed red with henna; drummers attend, a mob soon collects, the news of the animal's size and fatness soon spreads, and all run to buy. The colouring of the horns is effected by applying the green leaves of the henna tree, bruised into a kind of poultice. Near the shambles is a number of cook-shops in the open air; each consisting merely of a wood fire, stuck round with wooden skewers, on which small bits of fat and lean meat, alternately mixed, and scarcely larger than a penny piece each, are roasting. Every thing looks very clean and comfortable; and a woman does the honours of the table, with a mat dish-cover on her knees, from which she serves her guests, who are squatted around her. Ground gussub water is retailed at hand, to those who can afford this beverage at their repast: the price, at most, does not exceed twenty cowries, or about two farthings and four-tenths of a farthing, English money, estimating the dollar at five shillings. Those who have houses eat at home; women never resort to cook-shops, and even at home eat apart from men.

The interior of the market is filled with stalls of bamboo, laid out in regular streets; where the more costly wares are sold, and articles of dress, and other little matters of use or ornament made and repaired. Bands of musicians parade up and down to attract purchasers to particular booths. Here are displayed coarse writing paper, of French manufacture, brought from Barbary; scissors and knives, of native workmanship; crude antimony and tin, both the produce of the country; unwrought silk of a red colour, which they make into belts and slings, or weave in strips into the finest cotton tobes; armlets and bracelets of brass; beads of glass, coral and amber; finger rings of pewter, and a few silver trinkets, but none of gold; tobes, turkadees, and turban shawls; coarse woollen cloths of all colours; coarse calico; Moorish dresses; the cast-off gaudy garbs of the Mamelukes of Barbary; pieces of Egyptian linen, checked or striped with gold; sword blades from Malta, &c., &c. The market is crowded from sunrise to sunset every day, not excepting their Sabbath, which is kept on Friday. The merchants understand the benefits of monopoly as well as any people in the world; they take good care never to overstock the market, and if anything falls in price, it is immediately withdrawn for a few days.—The market is regulated with the greatest fairness, and the regulations are strictly and impartially enforced. If a tobe or turkadee, purchased here, is carried to Bornou or any other distant place, without being opened, and is there discovered to be of inferior quality, it is immediately sent back, as a matter of course, the name of the *dyala*, or broker, being written inside every parcel. In this case the *dyala* must find out the seller, who, by the laws of Kano, is forthwith obliged to refund the purchase money.

HUGH CLAPPERTON
Travels in Africa, 1826

72

LEARNED PIGS

It was to King's Cross fair that I moved from Stepney with my conjuring show, and very well I did with it, in spite of counter-attractions—and there were many—especially in the way of performing animals, such as fortune-telling ponies and 'learned pigs'.

The latter animals were just then very popular, the public being amazed at the idea that creatures generally considered so stupid should perform tricks such as picking out cards, that seemingly called for an exercise of unusual intelligence. Well, all animals have intelligence of a kind, and, in regard to the learned pig, I will explain how, by the craft of the showman, his small intelligence can be made to take on an air of real scholarship. 'How simple!' you will say when you know how it's done. Quite so; but it is not everybody who knows how to utilise properly these simple things, otherwise the show business would be overcrowded.

Well, now, the making of a learned pig is upon this wise. You get your pig, fat and comfortable-looking and not too old, a fairly long stout stick, a leather strap that will buckle neatly round the pig's neck and has also a small plate and screw rivet that will attach it to the stick. Then you are ready to commence the lessons.

In the end of the stick, not the end to which the strap is attached, you bore a hole, and through this drive a long nail into the floor of your academy so that the stick can move freely round on it in a circle, but in no other way. When the pig's neck is buckled into the strap at the other end of the stick the animal is bound to move in a circle, of which the nailed end of the stick is the centre.

Then with a little cane to direct his movements you induce the pig to walk. Of course he goes round and round and round, for he can move in no other direction, and when he wants to stop, which is often, you just keep him going by gentle taps with the cane. When you have kept him walking round some time you begin to let him stop in his course now and again, but always just before the stop giving a slight click with the fingers. The slightest sound will do, merely the snap of the thumb-nail against the finger-nail is sufficient. The pig will hear it, and in a very short time will stop anywhere in his monotonous walk directly he hears the slight signal.

You then vary the lesson by arranging a pack of cards face upwards just outside the circle, fixed, of course, by the length of the stick, which the pig traverses, and commence to patter as if to an audience somewhat in this style: 'Well, Toby, you see the cards before you. Which is the ace of spades?' Any card you like you can, of course, name. Round goes the pig in his circle, and as he comes opposite the card 'click' go your nails, and he at once stops.

'You see, ladies and gentlemen,' you proceed, 'Toby knows the cards. Will someone kindly name a card they would like to pick out.' Round goes piggy as you patter, and 'click,' you stop him where you like. In two or three days the pig, without the stick or the strap, will commence to move round at a tap from your switch whenever a circle of cards or persons is formed. He will also stop dead at the finger-click until the touch of the switch lets him know he must move on again. Then his education is complete.

You can then send him round a circle of people, asking him to pick out the man that likes kissing the girls. In fact, vary your entertainment as you will, the pig will be listening for the 'click,' not to your patter, and will stop directly he hears it, while the audience will not notice the slight sound. With every performance the pig will improve, especially if you accustom him to receive after each show an apple, potato, or some such little luxury.

I have seen first-class learned pigs trained in a week by this simple method. Their intelligence consists almost entirely in having a sharp ear for the 'click' that brings them a welcome stop in their walk. The rest of the performance that so amazes the onlookers is due to the showman's arrangement of his cards, his audience, and his patter.

In my long life I have found many wonderful things, besides the performance of the learned pig, whose entire art and mystery consists of a quick ear and a nimble tongue, and incidentally, as you will discover if you follow my story, have profited thereby.

'LORD' GEORGE SANGER

Seventy Years a Showman, 1910

73

BEGGARS IN AMERICA

AMERICAN beggars knock boldly at doors like kings' messengers. An imposing mansion with marble pillars is a challenge to them, and they dance up its steps and press the button of an electric bell with a violence that no familiar friends of the house would dare use; but an English beggar almost sinks into the earth when his ears receive the report of his own timid hand. In fact, except in very rare instances, where a large house has been approached and—for a wonder—found good, and has become famous to the begging fraternity—except in these very rare instances, English beggars pass by large mansions as though they were empty churches or smallpox hospitals.

I don't suppose there is a more daring or more impudent rascal on earth than a good American beggar. It is always his boast that he has begged an ex-president, or the present one, and he claims to have received benefits from a number of well-known millionaires, actors, and prize-fighters. Such proud experiences never fall from the lips of an English beggar, for the simple reason that he lives on the working and middle classes. A row of small cottages is of more benefit to him than an equal number of fine villas, and he thinks he is in a hungry wilderness when there is nothing to be seen but very large houses—and he is quite right.

It has always seemed strange to me that Americans, who as a race are notoriously eager to make money, should be so generous to a beggar. Even when they refuse it is often more on account of haste than meaness. Not only that, but they give with so much indifference, and are never annoyed at being solicited, whether they are reading papers on the verandahs of hotels, or promenading a sea-beach in the presence of ladies. And, what is more, they seldom pry into a beggar's past, except in such cases where their interest is aroused by a beggar's speech. For instance, a gentleman's father or mother may have been English, Irish or Scotch, and when he thinks he can detect that tongue in the speech of a beggar, he is very apt to ask one or two questions, and the beggar is invariably more generously assisted.

The American tramp begs in such a quick, thorough, business-like manner, with such calm persistence and with such confidence, that he must at last meet with success in the very worst places; for that reason he will not stand for cross-examination, and if people attempt to pry into his life, he is just as likely as not to tell them straight that he is a beggar, that he does not work, and never will.

W. H. DAVIES
The Adventures of Johnny Walker, 1926

74

SUBJECTIVE COLOURS

On the evening of the 12th of July I reached Chamouni; the weather was not quite clear, but it was promising; white cumuli had floated round Mont Blanc during the day, but these diminished more and more, and the light of the setting sun was of that lingering rosy hue which bodes good weather. Two parallel beams of a purple tinge were drawn by the shadows of the adjacent peaks, straight across the Glacier des Bossons, and the Glacier des Pélerins was also steeped for a time in the same purple light. Once when the surrounding red illumination was strong, the shadows of the Grands Mulets falling upon the adjacent snow appeared of a *vivid green*.

This green belonged to the class of *subjective* colours, or colours produced by contrast, about which a volume might be written. The eye received the impression of green, but the colour was not external to the eye. Place a red wafer on white paper, and look at it intently, it will be surrounded in a little time by a green fringe: move the wafer bodily away, and the entire space which it occupied upon the paper will appear green. A body may have its proper colour entirely masked in this way. Let a red wafer be attached to a piece of red glass, and from a moderately illuminated position let the sky be regarded through the glass; the wafer will appear of a vivid green. If a strong beam of light be sent through a red glass and caused to fall upon a screen, which at the same time is moderately illuminated by a separate source of white light, an opaque body placed in the path of the beam will cast a green shadow upon the screen which may be seen by several hundred persons at once. If a blue glass be used, the shadow will be yellow, which is the complementary colour to blue.

When we suddenly pass from open sunlight to a moderately illuminated room, it appears dark at first, but after a little time the eye regains the power of seeing objects distinctly. Thus one effect of light upon the eye is to render it less sensitive, and light of any particular colour falling upon the eye blunts its appreciation *of that colour*. Let us apply this to the shadow upon the screen. This shadow is moderately illuminated by a jet of white light; but the space surrounding it is red, the effect of which is to *blind* it in some degree to the perception of red. Hence, when the feeble white light of the shadow reaches the eye, the red component of this light is, as it were, abstracted from it, and the eye sees the residual colour, which is green. A similar explanation applies to the shadows of the Grands Mulets.

JOHN TYNDALL
The Glaciers of the Alps, 1860

75

DEFORESTATION

THE wastefulness of man is very pronounced at the present period of history. He is, as we have seen, using up his capital —of 'bottled sunlight' in the shape of coal, of other stored carbon like oil, of stored nitrates and phosphates—far faster than it was accumulated by nature. He is doing just the same sort of thing with regard to forests, wild animals, and even soil. Forests are cut down to provide wood for fuel and paper-making, but mostly to clear the land for crops or grazing. Sometimes the face of a country is entirely changed by the destruction of forests. Over huge areas of China, for example, there is not a tree to be seen except a few ornamental ones in gardens. There is no firewood for fuel, and as there is no coal available for the common people, they have to burn refuse.

When forests are cut down, provision is rarely made for replanting on a proper scale. Some countries have taken steps about this. In the United States, big areas have been proclaimed forest reserves. In countries like Germany and Switzerland, many cities and parishes have their own forests which are kept up so as to yield a steady income. In this country the Forestry Commission is planting hundreds of thousands of trees on waste land. But unless similar steps are taken by all main forest countries, there will be a world shortage of wood in a very few generations.

The cutting down of forests may also be very bad for the soil. Where hills or mountains are covered with trees, the water that falls as rain cannot run off quickly. The shade of the trees prevents it evaporating quickly and the soil holds it like a sponge, only allowing it to trickle down gradually. But if the forests are cut down, the soil is no longer protected by their foliage nor held together by their roots, and after a time is washed away. Then when rain falls, there is nothing to hold it back, and it all runs off quickly, eroding the surface still further, and pouring down to the lowlands in torrents. Even if exactly the same amount of rain as before falls on the hills they will now be dry and barren, because it runs away so quickly. And instead of the lowlands receiving a steady supply of water in the streams and rivers from the hills, most of the water will come down in the form of dangerous floods, while the rest of the time there will be too little water.

The mountains along the coast of Illyria and Dalmatia are good examples of these disastrous effects of reckless cutting of forests. In many parts of Africa, too, deforestation has had serious results. In some parts of Kenya and Tanganyika the soil has been almost entirely washed away, leaving only bare rock, and the occasional torrents from the rains make the streams cut deep bare gorges into the countryside instead of pleasant little valleys full of vegetation. In all such cases replanting of trees in the right situation ought to be done at once. But even then it will take a very long time for the soil to form again.

E. N. da C. ANDRADE and JULIAN HUXLEY
Earth and Man, 1935

III. IDEAS AND OPINIONS

76

THE LONDONER

I WAS born, as you have heard, in a crowd. This has begot in me an entire affection for that way of life, amounting to an almost insurmountable aversion from solitude and rural scenes. This aversion was never interrupted or suspended, except for a few years in the younger part of my life, during a period in which I had set my affections upon a charming young woman. Every man while the passion is upon him, is for a time at least addicted to groves and meadows and purling streams. During this short period of my existence, I contracted just familiarity enough with rural objects to understand tolerably well ever after the *poets*, when they declaim in such passionate terms in favour of a country life.

For my own part, now the fit is past, I have no hesitation in declaring, that a mob of happy faces crowding up at the pit door of Drury-lane Theatre, just at the hour of six, gives me ten thousand sincerer pleasures, than I could ever receive from all the flocks of silly sheep that ever whitened the plains of Arcadia or Epsom Downs.

This passion for crowds is nowhere feasted so full as in London. The man must have a rare *recipe* for melancholy, who can be dull in Fleet Street. I am naturally inclined to hypochondria, but in London it vanishes, like all other ills. Often, when I have felt a weariness or distaste at home, have I rushed out into her crowded Strand, and fed my humour, till tears have wetted my cheek for unutterable sympathies with the multitudinous moving picture, which she never fails to present at all hours, like the scenes of a shifting pantomime.

The very deformities of London, which give distaste to

others, from habit do not displease me. The endless succession of shops where *Fancy miscalled Folly* is supplied with perpetual gauds and toys, excite in me no puritanical aversion. I gladly behold every appetite supplied with its proper food. The obliged customer, and the obliging tradesman—things which live by bowing, and things which exist but for homage—do not affect me with disgust; from habit I perceive nothing but urbanity, where other men, more refined, discover meanness: I love the very smoke of London, because it has been the medium most familiar to my vision. I see grand principles of honour at work in the dirty ring which encompasses two combatants with fists, and principles of no less eternal justice in the detection of a pick-pocket. The salutary astonishment with which an execution is surveyed, convinces me more forcibly than a hundred volumes of abstract polity, that the universal instinct of man in all ages has leaned to order and good government.

CHARLES LAMB
first published, 1802

77

WHY I COULD NEVER LIVE IN LONDON

WHEN I am asked whether I should like to live in London, invariably I reply without thinking: 'I should hate it,' and, if my questioner asks the reason, I say, again without thinking: 'Because it's a dirty, stinking, noisy, overcrowded place.' Now that I am trying to set down the true reasons for my dislike of town life, I find these thoughtless answers to be correct and sufficient.

Those four adjectives provide the main reasons why our foremost city holds few attractions for me. Take the first two of them—dirty and stinking. Isn't the country dirty and stinking, you will ask? Yes, but rural dirt and rural stinks are clean and wholesome compared with those of London—those petrol-scented streets, the fetid stench of hot, hurrying humanity, and over all the grime, grime unspeakable, London's grime, from which there is no escape. Country mud and the smell of the byre are pleasing things by comparison.

Noisy! It's one eternal grinding roar, all day long, all night long, above ground and below. Hideous mechanical monstrosities striving endlessly to get somewhere—where or why they do not know; neither do their drivers nor their passengers, but they go on and on, round and round, unceasingly—a mechanical maelstrom which the twentieth century has wound up, and knows not how to stop. Pity the rural dweller who gets caught up in this insane whirligig even for one twenty-four hours, for all night long the slaves of London continue their noise in preparation for the morrow's crazy turmoil.

They broke all the crockery in London underneath my window the other night—at least that was what it sounded like. Apparently they brought the stuff in car loads, and backed it under my window before they smashed it. At intervals I could hear the buzz of an engine, the gnashing of bad-tempered gear-changing, and a raucous voice bellowing 'On the other lock,' and similar directions, interspersed with many profanities. At the time I could have witnessed with great pleasure the owner of that voice stretched upon a medieval rack.

But the fourth and last adjective, overcrowded, is the chief reason for my dislike of London. People, people, people everywhere, all rushing about, obsessed with this modern craze for speed at all costs. At one point they descend into the earth, and at another they are spewed up, London's vomit, all panting, rushing, hurrying. Not content with their mechanical aids to speed, the escalators, some run down them, and others, incredible though it seems, run up them. Poor devils! How dull their lives must be, for they can never stop to think. Slaves they are of London life, and as such they are to be pitied. The farm labourer, whom many of these town slaves affect to despise, is not driven in this fashion. The Londoner lives, as they say in the army, by numbers; the rural dweller does the same thing, but judging his own time, and, it is to be hoped, thanking his Maker for the privilege.

A. G. STREET

Hedge-Trimmings, 1933

78

WALKING TOURS

Now, to be properly enjoyed, a walking tour should be gone upon alone. If you go in a company, or even in pairs, it is no longer a walking tour in anything but name; it is something else and more in the nature of a picnic. A walking tour should be gone upon alone, because freedom is of the essence; because you should be able to stop and go on, and follow this way or that, as the freak takes you; and because you must have your own pace, and neither trot alongside a champion walker, nor mince in time with a girl. And then you must be open to all impressions and let your thoughts take colour from what you see. You should be as a pipe for any wind to play upon. "I cannot see the wit," says Hazlitt, "of walking and talking at the same time. When I am in the country I wish to vegetate like the country,"—which is the gist of all that can be said upon the matter. There should be no cackle of voices at your elbow, to jar on the meditative silence of the morning. And so long as a man is reasoning he cannot surrender himself to that fine intoxication that comes of much motion in the open air, that begins in a sort of dazzle and sluggishness of the brain, and ends in a peace that passes comprehension.

ROBERT LOUIS STEVENSON
Virginibus Puerisque, 1881

79

GOING FOR A WALK

It is a fact that not once in all my life have I gone out for a walk. I have been taken out for walks; but that is another matter. Even while I trotted prattling by my nurse's side I regretted the good old days when I had, and wasn't, a perambulator. When I grew up it seemed to me that the one advantage of living in London was that nobody ever wanted me to come out for a walk. London's very drawbacks—its endless noise and hustle, its smoky air, the squalor ambushed everywhere in it—assured this one immunity. Whenever I was with friends in the country, I knew that at any moment, unless rain were actually falling, some man might suddenly say "Come out for a walk!" in that sharp imperative tone which he would not dream of using in any other connexion. People seem to think there is something inherently noble and virtuous in the desire to go for a walk. Any one thus desirous feels that he has a right to impose his will on whomever he sees comfortably settled in an arm-chair, reading. It is easy to say simply "No" to an old friend. In the case of a mere acquaintance one wants some excuse. "I wish I could, but"—nothing ever occurs to me except "I have some letters to write." This formula is unsatisfactory in three ways. (1) It isn't believed. (2) It compels you to rise from your chair, go to the writing-table, and sit improvising a letter to somebody until the walkmonger (just not daring to call you liar and hypocrite) shall have lumbered out of the room. (3) It won't operate on Sunday mornings. "There's no post out till this evening" clinches the matter; and you may as well go quietly.

Walking for walking's sake may be as highly laudable and exemplary a thing as it is held to be by those who practise it. My objection to it is that it stops the brain. Many a man has professed to me that his brain never works so well as when he is swinging along the high road or over hill and dale. This boast is not confirmed by my memory of anybody who on a Sunday morning has forced me to partake of his adventure. Experience teaches me that whatever a fellow-guest may have of power to instruct or amuse when he is sitting on a chair, or standing on a hearth-rug, quickly leaves him when he takes me out for a walk. The ideas that came so thick and fast to him in any room, where are they now? where that encyclopedic knowledge which he bore so lightly? where the kindling fancy that played like summer lightning over *any* topic that was started? The man's face that was so mobile is set now; gone is the light from his fine eyes. He says that A. (our host) is a thoroughly good fellow. Fifty yards further on, he adds that A. is one of the best fellows he has ever met. We tramp another furlong or so, and he says that Mrs. A.

is a charming woman. Presently he adds that she is one of the most charming women he has ever known. We pass an inn. He reads vapidly aloud to me: "The King's Arms. Licensed to sell Ales and Spirits." I foresee that during the rest of the walk he will read aloud any inscription that occurs. We pass a milestone. He points at it with his stick and says "Uxminster. 11 miles." We turn a sharp corner at the foot of a hill. He points at the wall, and says "Drive slowly." I see far ahead, on the other side of the hedge bordering the high road, a small notice-board. He sees it too. He keeps his eye on it. And in due course "Trespassers," he says, "Will be Prosecuted." Poor man!—mentally a wreck.

MAX BEERBOHM
And Even Now, 1920

80

THE MISFORTUNES OF OTHERS

I AM convinced we have a degree of delight, and that no small one, in the real misfortunes and pains of others; for let the affection be what it will in appearance, if it does not make us shun such objects, if on the contrary it induces us to approach them, if it makes us dwell upon them, in this case I conceive we must have a delight or pleasure of some species or other in contemplating objects of this kind. Do we not read the authentic histories of scenes of this nature with as much pleasure as romances or poems, where the incidents are fictitious? The prosperity of no empire, nor the grandeur of no king, can so agreeably affect in the reading as the ruin of the state of Macedon, and the distress of its unhappy prince. Such a catastrophe touches us in history as much as the destruction of Troy does in fable. Our delight, in cases of this kind, is very greatly heightened if the sufferer be some excellent person who sinks under an unworthy fortune. Scipio and Cato are both virtuous characters; but we are more deeply affected by the violent death of the one, and the ruin of the great cause he adhered to, than with the deserved triumphs and uninterrupted prosperity of the other; for terror is a passion which always produces delight when it does not press too close; and pity is a passion accompanied with pleasure, because it arises from love and social affection.

EDMUND BURKE
Of the Sublime and Beautiful, 1756

81

PRISONERS

THE general prevalence and spread of wickedness in prisons, and abroad by the discharged prisoners, will now be as easily accounted for as the propagation of disease. It is often said, "A prison pays no debts"; I am sure it may be added, that a prison mends no morals. Sir John Fielding observes that "a criminal discharged—generally by the next sessions, after the execution of his comrades, becomes the head of a gang of his own raising": —improved, no doubt, in skill by the company he kept in gaol. And petty offenders who are committed to bridewell for a year or two, and spend that time, not in hard labour, but in idleness and wicked company, or are sent for that time to county gaols, generally grow desperate, and come out fitted for the perpetration of any villainy. Half the robberies committed in and about London are planned in the prisons by that dreadful assemblage of criminals and the number of idle people who visit them. How contrary this to the intention of our laws with regard to petty offenders; which certainly is to correct and reform them! Instead of which, their confinement doth notoriously promote and increase the very vices it was designed to suppress. Multitudes of young creatures, committed for some trifling offence, are totally ruined there. I make no scruple to affirm that if it were the wish and aim of magistrates to effect the destruction present and future of young delinquents, they could not devise a more effectual method than to confine them so long in our prisons, those seats and seminaries (as they have been very properly called) of idleness and every vice.

Shall these irregularities, the sources of misery, disease, and wickedness, be endured in a nation celebrated for good sense and humanity; and who from these principles do treat one sort of prisoners with tenderness and generosity? I mean prisoners of war. These have provision in plenty; some to spare and sell to the soldiers on guard; we frequently saw their stated allowance hung up for their inspection. Some prisons have large areas for them to walk in; and at night every man had a hammock to himself. It is the farthest thing in the world from my wish to deprive captives of any one of these benefits—I am only desirous of seeing the same humanity shown to our countrymen in distress: so that a consistent and uniform practice may prove our benevolence to be a firm and steady principle; and that those who are censorious may find no occasion for ascribing our kind usage of foreigners to a less amiable motive.

Here it will be said, prisoners of war are not felons, nor yet debtors; and government is sometimes, at the end of a war, reimbursed the expense of maintaining them. This latter I believe is fact; and the former is true without dispute: we do not look upon foreign enemies, nor they upon us, as either debtors or felons: we cut one another to pieces in battle, but when that is over we grow cool and compassionate. I grant there is a material difference in the circumstances of foreign and domestic prisoners, but there is none in their nature. Debtors and felons, as well as hostile foreigners, are men, and by men they ought to be treated as men.

Those gentlemen who, when they are told of the misery which our prisoners suffer, content themselves with saying, Let them take care to keep out, prefaced perhaps with an angry prayer, seem not duly sensible of the favour of Providence which distinguishes them from the sufferers: they do not remember that we are required to imitate our gracious Heavenly Parent, who is kind to the unthankful, and to the evil: they also forget the vicissitudes of human affairs; the unexpected changes to which men are liable: and that those whose circumstances are affluent may in time be reduced to indigence, and become debtors and prisoners. And as to criminality, it is possible that a man who has often shuddered at hearing the account of a murder, may on a sudden temptation commit that very crime. Let him that thinks he standeth take heed lest he fall, and commiserate those that are fallen.

JOHN HOWARD
The State of the Prisons, 1777

82

THE WAR OF JENKINS' EAR

THE conduct of Walpole with regard to the Spanish war is the great blemish of his public life. Archdeacon Coxe imagined that he had discovered one grand principle of action to which the whole public conduct of his hero ought to be referred. "Did the administration of Walpole," says the biographer, "present any uniform principle which may be traced in every part, and which gave combination and consistency to the whole? Yes, and that principle was, THE LOVE OF PEACE." It would be difficult, we think, to bestow a higher eulogium on any statesman. But the eulogium is far too high for the merits of Walpole. The great ruling principle of his public conduct was indeed a love of peace, but not in the sense in which Archdeacon Coxe uses the phrase. The peace which Walpole sought was not the peace of the country, but the peace of his own administration. During the greater part of his public life, indeed, the two objects were inseparably connected. At length he was reduced to the necessity of choosing between them, of plunging the state into hostilities for which there was no just ground, and by which nothing was to be got, or of facing a violent opposition in the country, in Parliament, and even in the royal closet. No person was more thoroughly convinced than he of the absurdity of the cry against Spain. But his darling power was at stake, and his choice was soon made. He preferred an unjust war to a stormy session. It is impossible to say of a Minister who acted thus that the love of peace was the one grand principle to which all his conduct was to be referred. The governing principle of his conduct was neither love of peace nor love of war, but love of power.

THOMAS BABINGTON MACAULAY
Essay on Horace Walpole, 1833

83

THE EFFECTS OF PARTY GOVERNMENT

REVOLVE, my Lord[1], our history from the Conquest. We scarcely ever had a prince who by fraud or violence had not made some infringement on the constitution. We scarcely ever had a parliament which knew, when it attempted to set limits to the royal authority, how to set limits to its own. Evils we have had continually calling for reformation, and reformations more grievous than any evils. Our boasted liberty sometimes trodden down, sometimes giddily set up, and ever precariously fluctuating and unsettled; it has only been kept alive by the blasts of continual feuds, war, and conspiracies. In no country in Europe has the scaffold so often blushed with the blood of its nobility. Confiscations, banishments, attainders, executions, make a large part of the history of such of our families as are not utterly extinguished by them. Formerly indeed things had a more ferocious appearance than they have at this day. In these early and unrefined ages, the jarring parts of a certain chaotic constitution supported their several pretensions by the sword. Experience and policy have since taught other methods.

At nunc res agitur tenui pulmone rubetae.

But how far corruption, venality, the contempt of honour, the oblivion of all duty to our country, and the most abandoned public prostitution are preferable to the more glaring and violent effects of faction, I will not presume to determine. Sure I am that they are very great evils.

EDMUND BURKE
A Vindication of Natural Society, 1756

[1] Bolingbroke.

84

FREEDOM

ITALY suffered a long period of governmental tyranny under the Fascist regime, which terminated in the frightful disaster and most cruel suffering which has befallen the Italian people. She would be very unwise to let herself again fall into the clutches of the Fascist totalitarian system in any guise in which it might present itself.

Such systems of governmental tyranny breed in conditions of social dislocation, economic hardship, and moral depression which follow in the wake of war and defeat. It is at such a crisis in their history that people should be most on their guard against unscrupulous parties seeking after power and most zealous in the preservation of their liberties.

When a nation has allowed itself to fall into a tyrannical regime, it cannot be absolved from the faults due to the guilt of that regime, and naturally we cannot forget the circumstances of Mussolini's attack on France and Great Britain when we were at our weakest, and the people thought that Great Britain would sink for ever—which, in fact, she has not done.

But in the main, speaking for the British—although the other victorious allies would have a say in this—I believe that the British nation will be happy to see the day when Italy, once again free and progressive, takes her place among all the peace-loving nations.

It has been said that the price of freedom is eternal vigilance. The question arises, "What is freedom?" There are one or two quite simple, practical tests by which it can be known in the modern world in peace conditions—namely:

Is there the right to free expression of opinion and of opposition and criticism of the Government of the day?

Have the people the right to turn out a Government of which they disapprove, and are constitutional means provided by which they can make their will apparent?

Are there courts of justice free from violence by the Executive and free of all threats of mob violence and all association with any particular political parties?

Will these courts administer open and well established laws which are associated in the human mind with the broad principles of decency and justice?

Will there be fair play for poor as well as for rich, for private persons as well as Government officials?

Will the rights of the individual, subject to his duties to the State, be maintained and asserted and exalted?

Is the ordinary peasant or workman, earning a living by daily toil and striving to bring up a family, free from the fear that some grim police organization under the control of a single party, like the *Gestapo*[1], started by the Nazi and Fascist parties, will tap him on the shoulder and pack him off without fair or open trial to bondage or ill-treatment?

These simple, practical tests are some of the title-deeds on which a new Italy could be founded.

WINSTON S. CHURCHILL

from a speech to the Italian people at Rome, August 28, 1944

85

COVETOUSNESS

I READ of late in an Act of Parliament; and this act made mention of an Act that was in King Henry's days, the third I trow it was; yea, and such another business there was in King Edward's time, the second also. In this Parliament that I speak of, the gentlemen and the commoners were at variance, as they were now of late. And there the gentlemen that were landlords would needs have away much lands from their tenants; and would needs have an Act of Parliament, that it might be lawful for them to inclose and make several from their tenants, and from the commons, such portions of their lands as they thought good. Much ado there was about this Act: at last it was concluded and granted that they might do so; provided alway, that they should leave sufficient to the tenant. Well; it was well that they were bound to leave

[1] German secret police under the Nazis.

sufficient for them. But who should be the judge to limit what was sufficient for them? Or who shall now judge what is sufficient? Well; I for my part cannot tell what is sufficient. But methought it was well that the tenants and poor commons should have sufficient. For if they had sufficient, thought I, they had cause to be quiet. And then fell I to make this argument within myself: if at that time it were put in their will and power that they might inclose, leaving to the tenant that were sufficient for him; if they had it then in their power, thought I, that they might this do, they would leave no more than sufficient. If they left to the tenants and poor commons no more in those days but sufficient; then if they had any more taken from them since that time, then had they now not sufficient.

They in Christ are equal with you. Peers of the realm must needs be. The poorest ploughman is in Christ equal with the greatest prince that is. Let them, therefore, have sufficient to maintain them, and to find them their necessaries. A plough-land must have sheep; yea, they must have sheep to dung their ground for bearing of corn; for if they have no sheep to help to fat the ground, they shall have but bare corn and thin. They must have swine for their food, to make their veneries or bacon of: their bacon is their venison, for they shall now have *hangum tuum*,[1] if they get any other venison; so that bacon is their necessary meat to feed on, which they may not lack. They must have other cattle: as horses to draw their plough, and for carriage of things to the markets; and kine for their milk and cheese, which they must live upon and pay their rents. These cattle must have pasture, which pasture if they lack, the rest must needs fail them: and pasture they cannot have, if the land be taken in, and inclosed from them. So, as I said, there was in both parts rebellion. Therefore, for God's love, restore their sufficient unto them, and search no more what is the cause of rebellion. But see and "beware of covetousness"; for covetousness is the cause of rebellion.

HUGH LATIMER

Last Sermon preached before King Edward VI, 1550

[1] a mock-Latin phrase coined by Latimer: 'they shall be hung if they try to get Venison by killing the lord's deer.'

86

RAILWAYS

THE sun had drawn landscapes for you—in green and blue and all imaginable colours, here in England. Not one of you ever looked at them then; not one of you cares for the loss of them now when you have shut the sun out with smoke. There was a rocky valley between Buxton and Bakewell, once upon a time, divine as the vale of Tempe; you might have seen the gods there, morning and evening—Apollo and all the sweet Muses of the light, walking in fair procession on the lawns of it, and to and fro among the pinnacles of its crags. You cared neither for gods nor grass, but for cash. You enterprised a railroad through the valley, you blasted its rock away, heaped thousands of tons of shale into its lovely stream. The valley is gone and the gods with it, and now every fool in Buxton can be at Bakewell in half an hour and every fool in Bakewell at Buxton; which you think is a lucrative process of exchange, you fools everywhere!

JOHN RUSKIN
Fors Clavigera, 1871-1887

87

WHY THE PYRAMIDS ?

"WE nave now," said Imlac, "gratified our minds with an exact view of the greatest work of man, except the wall of China.

"Of the wall it is very easy to assign the motive. It secured a wealthy and timorous nation from the incursions of barbarians, whose unskilfulness in arts made it easier for them to supply their wants by rapine than by industry, and who from time to time poured in upon the habitations of peaceful commerce, as vultures descend upon domestic fowl. Their celerity and fierceness made the wall necessary, and their ignorance made it efficacious.

"But for the pyramids no reason has ever been given adequate to the cost and labour of the work. The narrowness of the chambers proves that it could afford no retreat from enemies, and treasures might have been reposited at far less expense with equal security. It seems to have been erected only in compliance with that hunger of imagination which preys incessantly upon life, and must always be appeased by some employment. Those who have already all that they can enjoy, must enlarge their desires. He that has built for use, till use is supplied, must begin to build for vanity, and extend his plan to the utmost power of human performance, that he may not be soon reduced to form another wish.

"I consider this mighty structure as a monument of the insufficiency of human enjoyments. A king, whose power is unlimited, and whose treasures surmount all real and imaginary wants, is compelled to solace, by the erection of a Pyramid, the satiety of dominion and tastelessness of pleasures, and to amuse the tediousness of declining life, by seeing thousands labouring without end, and one stone, for no purpose, laid upon another. Whoever thou art, that, not content with a moderate condition, imaginest happiness in royal magnificence, and dreamest that command or riches can feed the appetite of novelty with perpetual gratifications, survey the Pyramids, and confess thy folly!"

SAMUEL JOHNSON
Rasselas, 1759

88
THE PYRAMIDS

I WENT to see and to explore the Pyramids.

Familiar to one from the days of early childhood are the forms of the Egyptian Pyramids, and now, as I approached them from the banks of the Nile, I had no print, no picture before me, and yet the old shapes were there; there was no change; they were just as I had always known them. I straightened myself in my stirrups, and strived to persuade my understanding that this was real Egypt, and that those angles which stood up between me and the West were of harder stuff, and more ancient than the paper pyramids of the green portfolio. Yet it was not till I came to the base of the great Pyramid that reality began to weigh upon my mind. Strange to say, the bigness of the distinct blocks of stones was the first sign by which I attained to feel the immensity of the whole pile. When I came, and trod, and touched with my hands, and climbed, in order that by climbing I might come to the top of one single stone, then, and almost suddenly, a cold sense and understanding of the Pyramid's enormity came down, overcasting my brain . . . . .

And Time too; the remoteness of its origin, no less than the enormity of its proportions, screens an Egyptian Pyramid from the easy and familiar contact of our modern minds; at its base the common earth ends, and all above is a world—one not created of God, not seeming to be made by men's hands, but rather the sheer giant-work of some old dismal age weighing down this younger planet.

Fine sayings! but the truth seems to be, after all, that the Pyramids are quite of this world; that they were piled up into the air for the realisation of some kingly crotchets about immortality, some priestly longing for burial fees; and that, as for the building, they were built like coral rocks by swarms of insects—by swarms of poor Egyptians, who were not only the abject tools and slaves of power, but who also ate onions for the reward of their immortal labours! The Pyramids are quite of this world.

ALEXANDER KINGLAKE
Eothen, 1844

89

LAUGHTER

HAVING mentioned laughing, I must particularly warn you against it: and I could heartily wish that you may often be seen to smile, but never heard to laugh while you live. Frequent and loud laughter is the characteristic of folly and ill manners: it is the manner in which the mob express their silly joy at silly things; and they call it being merry. In my mind there is nothjng so illiberal, and so illbred, as audible laughter. True wit, or sense, never yet made anybody laugh; they are above it: they please the mind, and give a cheerfulness to the countenance. But it is low buffoonery, or silly accidents, that always excite laughter; and that is what people of sense and breeding should show themselves above. A man's going to sit down, in the supposition that he had a chair behind him, and falling down upon his breech for want of one, sets a whole company a-laughing, when all the wit in the world would not do it; a plain proof, in my mind, how low and unbecoming a thing laughter is. Not to mention the disagreeable noise that it makes, and the shocking distortion of the face that it occasions. Laughter is easily restrained by a very little reflection; but, as it is generally connected with the idea of gaiety, people do not enough attend to its absurdity. I am neither of a melancholy, nor a cynical disposition; and am as willing, and as apt, to be pleased as anybody; but I am sure that, since I have had the full use of my reason, nobody has ever heard me laugh. Many people, at first from awkwardness and *mauvaise honte*,[1] have got a very disagreeable and silly trick of laughing whenever they speak: and I know a man of very good parts, Mr. Waller, who cannot say the commonest thing without laughing; which makes those, who do not know him, take him at first for a natural fool.

LORD CHESTERFIELD
Letter to His Son, 1748

90

CANT

MY dear friend, clear your *mind* of cant. You may *talk* as other people do: you may say to a man, "Sir, I am your most humble servant." You are *not* his most humble servant. You may say, "These are bad times; it is a melancholy thing to be reserved to such times." You don't mind the times. You tell a man, "I am sorry you had such bad weather the last day of your journey, and were so much wet." You don't care sixpence whether he is wet or dry. You may *talk* in this manner; it is a mode of talking in society: but don't *think* foolishly.

SAMUEL JOHNSON to James Boswell, 1783
Boswell's *Life of Johnson*

[1] bashfulness.

91

HONOUR

(FALSTAFF, the fat knight, talks to Prince Hal before the Battle of Shrewsbury.)

Falstaff

Hal, if thou seest me down in the battle, and bestride me, so; 'tis a point of friendship.

Prince Hal

Nothing but a colossus can do thee that friendship. Say thy prayers, and farewell.

Falstaff

I would 'twere bed-time, Hal, and all well.

Prince Hal

Why, thou owest God a death. *Exit.*

Falstaff

'Tis not due yet; I would be loath to pay him before his day. What need I be so forward with him that he calls not on me? Well, 'tis no matter; honour pricks me on. Yea, but how if honour prick me off when I come on? how then? Can honour set to a leg? no: or an arm? no: or take away the grief of a wound? no. Honour hath no skill in surgery, then? no. What is honour? a word. What is in that word honour? air. A trim reckoning! Who hath it? he that died o' Wednesday. Doth he feel it? no. Doth he hear it? no. 'Tis insensible, then? yea, to the dead. But will it not live with the living? no. Why? detraction will not suffer it. Therefore I'll none of it. Honour is a mere scutcheon: and so ends my catechism.

Exit.

WILLIAM SHAKESPEARE
1 *Henry IV* 1596-7

92

A DUEL

(*Bob Acres, squire of Clod Hall, Devonshire, is about to challenge his rival to a duel. He has been egged on by the pugnacious Irishman,*

Sir Lucius O'Trigger. His servant David endeavours to dissuade him.)

David.

Then, by the mass, sir! I would do no such thing—ne'er a St. Lucius O'Trigger in the kingdom should make me fight, when I wasn't so minded. Oons! what will the old lady say, when she hears o't?

Acres

Ah! David, if you had heard Sir Lucius!—Odds sparks and flames! he would have roused your valour.

David

Not he, indeed. I hates such bloodthirsty cormorants. Look'ee, master, if you wanted a bout at boxing, quarter-staff, or short-staff, I should never be the man to bid you cry off: but for your curst sharps and snaps, I never knew any good come of 'em.

Acres

But my honour, David, my honour! I must be careful of my honour.

David

Ay, by the mass! and I would be very careful of it; and I think in return my honour couldn't do less than to very careful of me.

Acres

Odds blades! David, no gentleman will ever risk the loss of his honour!

David

I say, then, it would be but civil in honour never to risk the loss of a gentleman.—Look'ee, master, this honour seems to me to be a marvellous false friend: ay, truly, a very courtier-like servant. —Put the case, I was a gentleman (which, thank God, no one can say of me); well—my honour makes me quarrel with another gentleman of my acquaintance.—So—we fight. (Pleasant enough that!) Boh;—I kill him—(the more's my luck!) now, pray who gets the profit of it?—Why, my honour. But put the case that he kills me!—by the mass! I go to the worms, and my honour whips over to my enemy.

Acres

No, David—in that case!—odds crowns and laurels! your honour follows you to the grave.

David

Now, that's just the place where I could make a shift to do without it.

Acres

Zounds! David, you are a coward!—It doesn't become valour to listen to you.—What, shall I disgrace my ancestors? Think of that, David—think what it would be to disgrace my ancestors!

David

Under favour, the surest way of not disgracing them, is to keep as long as you can out of their company. Look'ee now, master, to go to them in such haste—with an ounce of lead in your brains—I should think might as well be let alone. Our ancestors are very good kind of folks; but they are the last people I should choose to have a visiting acqaintance with.

Acres

But, David, now, you don't think there is such very, very, very great danger, hey?—Odd's life! people often fight without any mischief done!

David

By the mass, I think 'tis ten to one against you!—Oons! here to meet some lion-hearted fellow, I warrant, with his damned double-barrelled swords, and cut-and-thrust pistols! Lord bless us! it makes me tremble to think o't—Those be such desperate bloody-minded weapons! Well, I never could abide 'em!—from a child I never could fancy 'em!—I suppose there an't been so merciless a beast in the world as your loaded pistol!

Acres

Zounds! I won't be afraid! Odds fire and fury! you shan't make me afraid.—Here is the challenge, and I have sent for my dear friend Jack Absolute to carry it for me.

David

Ay, i' the name of mischief, let him be the messenger.—For my part I wouldn't lend a hand to it for the best horse in your stable. By the mass! it don't look like another letter! It is, as I may say, a designing and malicious-looking letter; and I warrant smells of gun-powder like a soldier's pouch!—Oons! I wouldn't swear it mayn't go off!

Acres

Out, you poltroon! you han't the valour of a grasshopper.

David

Well, I say no more—'twill be sad news, to be sure, at Clod Hall! but I ha' done. How Phillis will howl when she hears of it!—Ah, poor bitch, she little thinks what shooting her master's going after! And I warrant old Crop, who has carried your honour, field and road, these ten years, will curse the hour he was born. (*Whimpering.*

Acres

It won't do, David—I am determined to fight—so get along, you coward, while I'm in the mind.

RICHARD BRINSLEY SHERIDAN
The Rivals, 1775

93

GOING TO CHURCH

I HAD rather ye should come of a naughty mind to hear the word of God for novelty, or for curiosity to hear some pastime, than to be away. I had rather ye should come as the tale is by the gentlewoman of London: one of her neighbours met her in the street, and said, "Mistress, whither go ye?" "Marry," said she, "I am going to St. Thomas of Acres to the sermon; I could not sleep all this last night, and I am going now thither; I never failed of a good nap there." And so I had rather ye should go a-napping to the sermons, than not to go at all. For with what mind soever ye come, though ye come for an ill purpose, yet peradventure ye may chance to be caught or ye go; the preacher may chance to catch you on his hook.

HUGH LATIMER
Sixth Sermon preached before King Edward VI, 1549

94

RELIGION AND THE INDUSTRIAL REVOLUTION

THE devout Christian, confronted with the spectacle of wrong and injustice, may draw either of two contrary conclusions. In the eyes of his religion the miner or weaver is just as important as the landlord or the cotton lord. Clearly, then, one will argue, it is the duty of a Christian State to prevent any class, however obscure and trivial its place in the world may seem to be, from sinking into degrading conditions of life. Every soul is immortal, and the consequence of ill-treatment and neglect in the brief day of its life on earth will be unending. If, therefore, society is so organised as to impose such conditions on any class, the Christian will demand the reform of its institutions. For such minds Christianity provides a standard by which to judge government, the industrial and economic order, the life of society, the way in which it distributes wealth and opportunities. This was the general standpoint of such a man as Shaftesbury.

But some minds drew a different moral from the equality that Christianity teaches. Every human soul is a reality, but the important thing about a human soul is its final destiny, and that destiny does not depend on the circumstances of this life. The world has been created on a plan of apparent injustice by a Providence that combined infinite power with infinite compassion. The arrangements that seem so capricious are really the work of that Power. But the same Power has given to the men and women who seem to live in such bitter and degrading surroundings, an escape from its cares by the exercise of their spiritual faculties. It is those faculties that make all men equal. Here they stand, in Marcus Aurelius's phrase, for a brief space between the two eternities, and no misery or poverty can prevent a soul from winning happiness in the world to come.

Thus whereas one man looking out on the chaos of the world calls for reform, the other calls for contemplation: one says, Who could tolerate such injustice? the other says, Who would not rejoice that there is another world? One says, Give these people the conditions of a decent life; the other says, Teach them to read the Bible.

J. L. HAMMOND AND BARBARA HAMMOND
The Town Labourer 1760-1832, 1917

95

HAPPINESS

I LAY it down as a maxim, that for a family to be happy, they must be well supplied with food and raiment. It is a sorry effort that people make to persuade others or to persuade themselves, that they can be happy in a state of want of the necessaries of life. The doctrines which fanaticism preaches, and which teach men to be content with poverty, have a very pernicious tendency, and are calculated to favour tyrants by giving them passive slaves. To live well, to enjoy all things that make life pleasant, is the right of every man who constantly uses his strength judiciously and lawfully. It is to blaspheme God to suppose that he created men to be miserable, to hunger, thirst, and perish with cold, in the midst of that abundance which is the fruit of their own labour. Instead, therefore, of applauding 'happy poverty,' which applause is so much the fashion of the present day, I despise the man that is poor and contented; for such content is a certain proof of a base disposition, a disposition which is the enemy of all industry, all exertion, all love of independence.

Let it be understood, however, that by poverty I mean real want, a real insufficiency of the food and lodging necessary to health and decency; and not that imaginary poverty, of which some persons complain. The man who, by his own and his family's labour, can provide a sufficiency of food and raiment, and a comfortable dwelling-place, is not a poor man. There must be different ranks and degrees in every civil society, and, indeed, so it is even amoungst the savage tribes. There must be different degrees of wealth; some must have more than others; and the richest must be a great deal richer than the least rich.

But it is necessary to the very existence of a people, that nine out of ten should live wholly by the sweat of their brow; and, is it not degrading to human nature, that all the nine-tenths should be called poor; and, what is still worse, call themselves poor, and be contented in that degraded state?

The laws, the economy, or management, of a state may be such as to render it impossible for the labourer, however skilful and industrious, to maintain his family in health and decency; and such has, for many years past, been the management of the affairs of this once truly great and happy land. A system of paper money, the effect of which was to take from the labourer the half of his earnings, was what no industry and care could make head against. I do not pretend that this system was adopted by design. But, no matter for the cause; such was the effect.

Better times, however, are approaching. The labourer now appears likely to obtain that hire of which he is worthy; and, therefore, this appears to me to be the time to press upon him the duty of using his best exertions for the rearing of his family in a manner that must give him the best security for happiness to himself, his wife and children, and to make him, in all respects, what his forefathers were. The people of England have been famed in all ages for their good living; for the abundance of their food, and goodness of their attire. The old sayings about English roast beef and plum-pudding, and about English hospitality, had not their foundations in *nothing*. And in spite of all refinements of sickly minds, it is *abundant living* amongst the people at large, which is the great test of good government, and the surest basis of national greatness and security.

WILLIAM COBBETT
Introduction to *Cottage Economy*, 1821

96

DEAD-ALIVE PEOPLE

EXTREME *busyness*, whether at school or college, kirk or market, is a symptom of deficient vitality; and a faculty for idleness implies a catholic appetite and a strong sense of personal identity. There is a sort of dead-alive, hackneyed people about, who are scarcely conscious of living except in the exercise of some conventional occupation. Bring these fellows into the country or set them aboard ship, and you will see how they pine for their desk or their study. They have no curiosity; they cannot give themselves over to random provocations; they do not take pleasure in the exercise of their faculties for its own sake; and unless Necessity lays about them with a stick, they will even stand still. It is no good speaking to such folk: they *cannot* be idle, their nature is not generous enough; and they pass those hours in a sort of coma, which are not dedicated to furious moiling in the gold-mill. When they do not require to go to office, when they are not hungry and have no mind to drink, the whole breathing world is a blank to them. If they have to wait an hour or so for a train they fall into a stupid trance with their eyes open. To see them, you would suppose there was nothing to look at and no one to speak with; you would imagine they were paralysed or alienated; and yet very possibly they are hard workers in their own way, and have good eyesight for a flaw in a deed or a turn of the market. They have been to school and college, but all the time they had their eye on the medal; they have gone about in the world and mixed with clever people, but all the time they were thinking of their own affairs. As if a man's soul were not too small to begin with, they have dwarfed and narrowed theirs by a life of all work and no play; until here they are at forty, with a listless attention, a mind vacant of all material of amusement, and not one thought to rub against another, while they wait for the train. Before he was breeched, he might have clambered on the boxes; when he was twenty, he would have stared at the girls; but now the pipe is smoked out, the snuff-box empty, and my gentleman sits bolt upright upon a bench, with lamentable eyes. This does not appeal to me as being Success in Life.

ROBERT LOUIS STEVENSON,
Virginibus Puerisque, 1881.

97

TOWNS AND THE INDUSTRIAL REVOLUTION

THE capital idea associated with towns and town life in history is the idea of shelter. Shelter first from the primitive dangers to mankind, nature, wild beasts, hostile tribes, robber barons. The town walls enclose a refuge where men and women can break or check the power of circumstances over their lives; a fortress where, relatively secure from want and violence, they can practise the arts of peace. As their wants multiply and their ambitions expand, their imagination is enriched, and the town comes to be the shelter not of life only, but of good life, protecting and fostering not only the food and homes of men and women, but light and knowledge, the humanity and culture that come from association and experiment, ideas of liberty and justice, the desire for experiment and self-expression. The town thus comes to symbolise the pride of man in his power, his initiative, his energy, his sympathy, the variety and character of his needs. To the people of ancient Athens, or of Florence or Siena in the twelfth and thirteenth century, or of Norwich or York in the fifteenth century, their town was not a mere roof from the wind and rain: it was a living personality, expressing and cherishing the instincts, tastes, beliefs, and corporate pride of the citizens, widely and richly pictured.

This city life had produced the art and literature of Greece and Italy, and in England a spirit of enterprise in representative government and public administration that influenced profoundly the form and development of our national institutions. The history of these towns, their brisk and eager life, their triumphs and their crimes, the active share that the citizens had taken in building, adorning, defending, and serving them, were reflected in their streets and halls and churches. The old English towns were often over-crowded, insanitary, honeycombed with alleys and courts that never saw the sun or breathed the air, but the fancy, and emotion, and the skill and craftsmanship of different ages, had made them beautiful and interesting. They were the home of a race, with all the traditions and pieties and heirlooms of a home.

It was of immense moment to the citizens of such towns whether their towns were beautiful, well governed, and administered with justice and magnanimity; this mattered much more to them than half the wars that have filled so disproportionate a page in the writing of history. It made just as great a difference to the people living under the shadow of the new industry whether Bolton and Oldham and Bradford and Manchester and Gateshead were beautiful or ugly, nobly or ignobly built and ruled. It made an even greater difference than would appear at first sight, for two reasons: England was still a country with very little government from the centre, and almost all the local responsibilities, health, housing, education, police, that are now subject to strict inspection and control, were left to the unchecked discretion and pleasure of magistrates and borough rulers. Parliament and Government knew nothing of this side of life. They passed no laws and exercised no supervision or initiative. The new industry had produced problems that were general, but except in respect of criminal law the central Government still looked upon them as local, and disclaimed all concern. The character of its local government and the success of its town life were therefore of even more engrossing concern to that population than they are to us today with our modern centralisation.

The form and appearance of the town were also of vital importance. There is a great chapter in Victor Hugo's *Notre Dame de Paris* describing the rise of printing and the overthrow of architecture as the principal language of mankind. But we have to remember that the population in the new industrial districts was a population for which literature scarcely existed, that the boundaries of their lives were for many the boundaries of their imagination, and the only things that spoke to their minds were the mill in which they worked and the town in which they lived. In their work they had none of the excitement or pleasure of handicraftsmen; they worked among ugly things, in ugly factories or ugly mines, for though an engine or a wheel may have a noble beauty and design, its beauty is obscured for those who are tending one small part of it and doing nothing else. Thus the monotonous strain of an occupation that gave no scope to the mind, and its unattractive setting, rendered them all the more dependent on their surroundings, making it more certain that they would derive from their buildings and their streets and their homes the spiritual influence that others would find in their work, and others again, by means of literature, in the imagination and experience of distant worlds and distant ages. The sights and sounds of his daily life affect every one, and they do not affect a person less because he receives few impressions from other sources.

J. L. HAMMOND and BARBARA HAMMOND
The Town Labourer 1760-1832, 1917

98

RICH AND POOR

THE most obvious division of society is into rich and poor; and it is no less obvious, that the number of the former bear a great disproportion to those of the latter. The whole business of the poor is to administer to the idleness, folly, and luxury of the rich; and that of the rich, in return, is to find the best methods of confirming the slavery and increasing the burdens of the poor. In a state of nature it is an invariable law that a man's acquisitions are in proportion to his labours. In a state of artifical society it is a law as constant and as invariable, that those who labour most, enjoy the fewest things; and that those who labour not at all, have the greatest number of enjoyments. A constitution of things this, strange and ridiculous beyond expression. We scarce believe a thing when we are told it, which we actually see before our eyes every day without being in the least surprised. I suppose that there are in Great Britain upwards of an hundred thousand people employed in lead, tin, iron, copper, and coal mines; these unhappy wretches scarce ever see the light of the sun; they are buried in the bowels of the earth; there they work at a severe and dismal task, without the least prospect of being delivered from it; they subsist upon the coarsest and worst sort of fare; they have their health miserably impaired, and their lives cut short, by being perpetually confined in the close vapour of these malignant minerals. An hundred thousand more at least are tortured without remission by the suffocating smoke, intense fires, and constant drudgery necessary in refining and managing the products of those mines. If any man informed us that two hundred thousand innocent persons were condemned to so intolerable slavery, how should we pity the unhappy sufferers, and how great would be our just indignation against those who inflicted so cruel and ignominious a punishment! This is an instance, I could not wish a stronger, of the numberless things which we pass by in their common dress, yet which shock us when they are nakedly represented.

EDMUND BURKE
A Vindication of Natural Society, 1756

99

A NATURAL ARISTOCRACY

A TRUE natural aristocracy is not a separate interest in the state, or separable from it. It is an essential integrant part of any large body rightly constituted. It is formed out of a class of legitimate presumptions, which taken as generalities, must be admitted for actual truths. To be bred in a place of estimation; to see nothing low and sordid from one's infancy; to be taught to respect oneself; to be habituated to the censorial inspection of the public eye; to look early to public opinion; to stand upon such elevated ground as to be enabled to take a large view of the widespread and infinitely diversified combinations of men and affairs in a large society; to have leisure to read, to reflect, to converse; to be enabled to draw the court and attention of the wise and learned wherever they are to be found;—to be habituated in armies to command and to obey; to be taught to despise danger in the pursuit of honour and duty; to be formed to the greatest degree of vigilance, foresight, and circumspection, in a state of things in which no fault is committed with impunity, and the slightest mistakes draw on the most ruinous consequences—to be led to a guarded and regulated conduct, from a sense that you are considered as an instructor of your fellow-citizens in their highest concerns, and that you act as a reconciler between God and man—to be employed as an administrator of law and justice, and to be thereby amongst the first benefactors of mankind—to be a professor of high science or of liberal and ingenuous art—to be amongst rich traders, who from their success are presumed to have sharp and vigorous understandings, and to possess the virtues of diligence, order, constancy, and regularity, and to have cultivated an habitual regard to commutative justice—these are the circumstances of men, that form what I should call a natural aristocracy, without which there is no nation.

EDMUND BURKE
An Appeal from the New to the Old Whigs, 1791

100

POETRY AND POLITICS

'Tis a vanity common to all writers to over-value their own productions; and 'tis better for me to own this failing in myself than the world to do it for me. For what other reason have I spent my life in so unprofitable a study? Why am I grown old in seeking so barren a reward as fame! The same parts and application which has made me a poet might have raised me to any honours of the gown which are often given to men of as little learning and less honesty than myself. No government has ever been, or ever can be, wherein time-servers and blockheads will not be uppermost. The persons are only changed, but the same jugglings in state, the same hypocrisy in religion, the same self-interest and mismanagement will remain for ever. Blood and money will be lavished in all ages, only for the preferment of new faces with old consciences. There is too often a jaundice in the eyes of great men; they see not those whom they raise in the same colours with other men. All whom they affect look golden to them, when the gilding is only in their own distempered sight. These considerations have given me a kind of contempt for those who have risen by unworthy ways. I am not ashamed to be little, when I see them so infamously great. Neither do I know why the name of poet should be dishonourable to me, if I am truly one, as I hope I am; for I will never do anything that shall dishonour it.

JOHN DRYDEN
Dedication to *Examen Poeticum*, 1693

101

CHAUCER

CHAUCER must have been a man of a most wonderful comprehensive nature, because, as it has been truly observed of him, he has taken into the compass of his *Canterbury Tales* the various manners and humours (as we now call them) of the whole English nation, in his age. Not a single character has escaped him. All his pilgrims are severally distinguished from each other; and not only in their inclinations, but in their very physiognomies and persons. Baptista Porta could not have described their natures better than by the marks which the poet gives them. The matter and manner of their tales and of their telling are so suited to their different educations, humours, and callings, that each of them would be improper in any other mouth. Even the grave and serious characters are distinguished by their several sorts of gravity: their discourses are such as belong to their age, their calling, and their breeding; such as are becoming of them, and of them only. Some of his persons are vicious, and some virtuous; some are unlearned or (as Chaucer calls them) lewd, and some are learned. Even the ribaldry of the low characters is different: the Reeve, the Miller, and the Cook are several men, and distinguished from each other, as much as the mincing lady Prioress and the broad-speaking gap-toothed Wife of Bath. But enough of this: there is such a variety of game springing up before me, that I am distracted in my choice, and know not which to follow. 'Tis sufficient to say, according to the proverb, that here is God's plenty. We have our forefathers and great-grandames all before us, as they were in Chaucer's days; their general characters are still remaining in mankind, and even in England, though they are called by other names than those of Monks, and Friars, and Canons, and Lady Abbesses, and Nuns: for mankind is ever the same, and nothing lost out of nature, though everything is altered.

JOHN DRYDEN
Preface to Fables, 1700

102

OF STUDIES

STUDIES serve for delight, for ornament, and for ability. Their chief use for delight is in privateness and retiring; for ornament, is in discourse; and for ability, is in the judgement and disposition of business. For expert men can execute, and perhaps judge of particulars, one by one; but the general counsels, and the plots and marshalling of affairs, come best from those that are learned. To spend too much time in studies is loth; to use them too much for ornament is affectation; to make judgement wholly by their rules is the humour[1] of a scholar. They perfect nature and are perfected by experience: for natural abilities are like natural plants, that need pruning by study; and studies themselves do give forth directions too much at large, except they be bounded in by experience. Crafty men condemn studies, simple men admire them, and wise men use them; for they teach not their own use; but that is a wisdom without them, and above them, won by observation. Read not to contradict and confute; nor to believe and take for granted; nor to find talk and discourse; but to weigh and consider.

Some books are to be tasted, others to be swallowed, and some few to be chewed and digested; that is, some books are to be read only in parts; others to be read, but not curiously;[2] and some few to be read wholly, and with diligence and attention. Some books also may be read by deputy, and extracts made of them by others; but that would be only in the less important arguments, and the meaner sort of books; else distilled books are like common distilled waters, flashy things. Reading maketh a full man;

[1] Disposition [2] in detail

conference a ready man; and writing an exact man. And therefore, if a man write little, he had need have a great memory; if he confer little, he had need have a present wit; and if he read little, he had need have much cunning, to seem to know that he doth not. Histories make men wise; poets witty; the mathematics subtle; natural philosophy deep; moral grave; logic and rhetoric able to contend. *Abeunt studia in mores.*[1] Nay there is no stond or impediment in the wit but may be wrought out by fit studies: like as diseases of the body may have appropriate exercises.

Bowling is good for the stone and reins; shooting for the lungs and breast; gentle walking for the stomach; riding for the head; and the like. So if a man's wit be wandering, let him study the mathematics; for in demonstrations, if his wit be called away never so little, he must begin again. If his wit be not apt to distinguish or find differences, let him study the schoolmen; for they are cymini sectores.[2] If he be not apt to beat over matters, and to call up one thing to prove and illustrate another, let him study the lawyers' cases. So every defect of the mind may have a special receipt.

FRANCIS BACON
Essays, 1597

103

ADDISON'S STYLE

HIS prose is the model of the middle style; on grave subjects not formal, on light occasions not groveling; pure without scrupulosity, and exact without apparent elaboration; always equable, and always easy, without glowing words or pointed sentences. Addison never deviates from his track to snatch a grace; he seeks no ambitious ornaments, and tries no hazardous innovations. His page is always luminous, but never blazes in unexpected splendour.

It was apparently his principal endeavour to avoid all harshness and severity of diction; he is therefore sometimes verbose in

[1] Reading affects character [2] i.e. hair splitters

his transitions and connections, and yet sometimes descends too much to the language of conversation; yet if his language had been less idiomatical, it might have lost somewhat of its genuine Anglicism. What he attempted, he performed; he is never feeble, and he did not wish to be energetic; he is never rapid, and he never stagnates. His sentences have neither studied amplitude, nor affected brevity: his periods, though not diligently rounded, are voluble and easy. Whoever wishes to attain an English style, familiar but not coarse, and elegant but not ostentatious, must give his days and nights to the volumes of Addison.

SAMUEL JOHNSON
Lives of the Poets, 1779-81

104

ON FAMILIAR STYLE

It is not easy to write a familiar style. Many people mistake a familiar for a vulgar style, and suppose that to write without affectation is to write at random. On the contrary, there is nothing that requires more precision, and, if I may say so, purity of expression, than the style I am speaking of. It utterly rejects not only all unmeaning pomp, but all low, cant phrases, and loose, unconnected, *slipshod* allusions. It is not to take the first word that offers, but the best word in common use; it is not to throw words together in any combinations we please, but to follow and avail ourselves of the true idiom of the language. To write a genuine familiar or truly English style, is to write as anyone would speak in common conversation, who had a thorough command and choice of words, or who could discourse with ease, force, and perspicuity, setting aside all pedantic and oratorical flourishes. Or to give another illustration, to write naturally is the same thing in regard to common conversation, as to read naturally is in regard to common speech. It does not follow that it is an easy thing to give the true accent and inflection to the words you utter, because you do not attempt to rise above the level of ordinary life and colloquial speaking. You do not assume indeed the solemnity of the pulpit, or the tone of stage-declamation: neither are you at liberty to gabble on at a venture, without emphasis or discretion, or to resort to vulgar dialect or clownish pronunciation. You must steer a middle course. You are tied down to a given and appropriate articulation, which is determined by the habitual associations between sense and sound, and which you can only hit by entering into the author's meaning, as you must find the proper words and style to express yourself by fixing your thoughts on the subject you have to write about. Any one may mouth out a passage with a theatrical cadence, or get upon stilts to tell his thoughts: but to write or speak with propriety and simplicity is a more difficult task. Thus it is easy to affect a pompous style, to use a word twice as big as the thing you want to express: it is not so easy to pitch upon the very word that exactly fits it. Out of eight or ten words equally common, equally intelligible, with nearly equal pretensions, it is a matter of some nicety and discrimination to pick out the very one, the preferableness of which is scarcely perceptible, but decisive.

The reason why I object to Dr. Johnson's style is that there is no discrimination, no selection, no variety in it. He uses none but "tall, opaque words," taken from the "first row of the rubric":—words with the greatest number of syllables, or Latin phrases with merely English terminations. If a fine style depended on this sort of arbitrary pretension, it would be fair to judge of an author's elegance by the measurement of his words, and the substitution of foreign circumlocutions (with no precise associations) for the mother-tongue. How simple it is to be dignified without ease, to be pompous without meaning! Surely, it is but a mechanical rule for avoiding what is low to be always pedantic and affected. It is clear you cannot use a vulgar English word, if you never use a common English word at all. A fine tact is shown in adhering to those which are perfectly common, and yet never falling into any expressions which are debased by disgusting circumstances or which owe their signification and point to professional or technical allusions. A truly natural or familiar style can never be quaint or vulgar, for this reason, that it is of universal force and applicability, and that quaintness and vulgarity arise out of the immediate connection of certain words with coarse and disagreeable, or with confined ideas. The last form what we understand by *cant* or *slang* phrases.

WILLIAM HAZLITT
Table Talk, 1821-4

105

STYLE

STYLE cannot be distinguished from matter. When a writer conceives an idea he conceives it in a form of words. That form of words constitutes his style, and it is absolutely governed by the idea. The idea can only exist in words, and it can only exist in one form of words. You cannot say exactly the same thing in two different ways. Slightly alter the expression, and you slightly alter the idea. Surely it is obvious that the expression cannot be altered without altering the thing expressed! A writer, having conceived and expressed an idea, may, and probably will, "polish it up". But what does he polish up? To say that he polishes up his style is merely to say that he is polishing up his idea, that he has discovered faults or imperfections in his idea, and is perfecting it.

An idea exists in proportion as it is expressed; it exists when it is expressed, and not before. It expresses itself. A clear idea is expressed clearly, and a vague idea vaguely. You need but take your own case and your own speech. For just as science is the development of common sense, so is literature the development of common daily speech. The difference between science and common sense is simply one of degree; similarly with speech and literature. Well, when you "know what you think", you succeed in saying what you think, in making yourself understood. When you "don't know what to think", your expressive tongue halts. And note how in daily life the characteristics of your style follow your mood; how tender it is when you are tender, how violent when you are violent. You have said to yourself in moments of emotion: "If only I could write . . ." etc. You were wrong. You ought to have said: "If only I could *think*—on this high plane."

When you have thought clearly you have never had any difficulty in saying what you thought, though you may occasionally have had some difficulty in keeping it to yourself. And when you cannot express yourself, depend upon it that you have nothing precise to express, and that what incommodes you is not the vain desire to express, but the vain desire to *think* more clearly. All this just to illustrate how style and matter are co-existent, and inseparable, and alike.

ARNOLD BENNETT
Literary Taste, 1909

BIOGRAPHICAL AND CRITICAL NOTES

1. WATER, WATER EVERYWHERE (*Captain Singleton*).

DANIEL DEFOE (1661 ?-1731), was a London merchant, a political pamphleteer and a writer of romantic stories of adventure, travel and fighting. The first of these, *Robinson Crusoe*, came out in 1719 when Defoe was nearly 60. It was an immediate success and proves that it is never too late in life to become a novelist.

Defoe held, and still holds, his readers' attention by his gift for making the tallest story seem true and the most unlikely situation real. He does this by a patient accumulation of detail and by a style so matter-of-fact, so candid and transparent, that it would seem impossible for an untruth to be concealed beneath it.

2. THIRST (*Travels in the Interior of Africa*).

MUNGO PARK (1771-1806) was a Scottish ship's surgeon who explored the river Niger. His *Travels*, published in 1799, were a modest and faithful account of one of the pioneering exploits in African discovery. In this passage the manly restraint with which he describes extreme suffering is admirable. His writing is honest and conscientious, and the whole of his book, which is not a long one, is wonderfully fascinating. He died in a fight with natives in a later expedition.

Later African travellers are Hugh Clapperton (Nos. 70, 71), David Livingstone (No. 13) and Sir Richard Burton (Nos. 23, 56, 57, 69).

3. GULLIVER AND THE LILLIPUTIANS (*Gulliver's Travels*).

JONATHAN SWIFT (1667-1745), though born and educated in Ireland, was of English descent. After a career as political writer, he became Dean of St. Patrick's in Dublin and a bitter champion of the Irish against English exploitation. He wrote many pamphlets and satires fiercely attacking the stupidity, prejudice and dishonesty he found in the society of his time. He was a man of keen intellect and great moral courage, essentially generous and a passionate spokesman of the oppressed; but disappointment and physical pain soured him and drove him mad.

His style is strong, forceful and clear; it is always perfectly suited to its subject. Here Swift is writing with the matter-of-fact, scientific detachment necessary to establish the "reality" of Gulliver's experiences. In this he may be compared with Defoe. *Gulliver's Travels* was a great and immediate success, and many of its first readers believed it to be true.

4. THE THAMES FROZEN (*Evelyn's Diary*).

JOHN EVELYN (1620-1706) was a royalist, a gentleman of independent means, and a writer on gardening, tree-cultivation, smoke-abatement, navigation and physical science. His *Diary* gives a vivid account of the life and personalities of his time.

5. THE GREAT FROST (*Orlando*).

VIRGINIA WOOLF (1882-1941) was a novelist, essayist and literary critic. Her novels are highly experimental. *Orlando* is an imaginative reconstruction of certain periods in English history, and the present extract deals with an occurrence in the Elizabethan period. Virginia Woolf's style is extremely studied: the words are chosen with infinite care, and the sentences are phrased and balanced like music. These qualities are even more marked in the other extract from her work (No. 32).

6. and 7. CLIMBING MONT BLANC AND THE DESCENT OF THE FINSTERAARHORN (*Glaciers of the Alps*).

JOHN TYNDALL (1820-1893) was a professor of natural history and wrote many scientific treatises, mostly on the study of physics. His books on mountaineering are written in the plain yet dignified style of the Victorian scientists at their best. It is the unpretentious writing of a man recording interesting experiences as faithfully as he can. See also Nos. 26 and 74, and compare the writing of Darwin (Nos. 36, 37, 67) and Dufferin (Nos. 30, 31, 68).

8. TRADING WITH NATIVES (*Captain Singleton*).

DANIEL DEFOE: see note on No. 1, p. 149

Notice again how Defoe makes a fictitious experience seem real.

9. STEALING CABBAGES (*Rural Rides*).

WILLIAM COBBETT (1762-1835) was the self-educated son of a small farmer. He became a soldier, a farmer, a political journalist and finally a Member of Parliament. He was imprisoned and exiled for his political opinions. He wrote the language of sturdy common-sense, despising all art and ornament. He fought the cause of the common man, whom he saw suffering great hardships under the growing power of industrialism. He hated many things, such as tea, taxes and snobbery; and he loved many others, like home-brewed beer, early rising, kindliness and independence. He was a violent political writer and speaker, but many contemporaries speak of the sweetness of his temper and disposition. His style is the reflection of his mind—honest, downright, vigorous, outspoken and pugnacious. (See also Nos. 41, 95).

10. THE GOOD SAMARITAN (*The Authorised Bible*).

WILLIAM TYNDALE (d. 1536) was the man mainly responsible for the translation of the New Testament which was the basis of the version produced in 1611 by a committee of 47 scholars and churchmen. This Authorised Version has been in use in the English Church ever since. Its prose is dignified, simple and moving. On the whole, the translators' preference was for words of Old English origin, though they had a sure instinct for the value of a longer word of Latin origin for the sake of emphasis or stateliness. (Consider the word "compassion" in this passage.) The style of the Bible is throughout free from affectation and obscurity; it never consciously strives after forced effects. This purity, no doubt due to the translators' reverence for their task, will instantly show up any shoddiness or affectation in our own or others' writing.

11. A WALK TO SALISBURY (*The Life of George Herbert*).

IZAAK WALTON (1593-1683) lived in an age of civil war and bitter religious and political controversy. Like other writers of his time—for example Andrew Marvell, the poet—Walton turned for relief to the charms of nature and the countryside. He is best known by his *Compleat Angler*, one of the most peaceful and reflective books in the language. He was the friend of several churchmen, and his life of the Church of England parson and poet, George Herbert, is one of his short biographies which are notable for their simplicity and sincerity and can be compared in style to the Authorised Bible.

12. SHOWMEN AT A FIRE (*Seventy Years A Showman*).

"LORD" GEORGE SANGER (1825-1910) wrote his entertaining and exciting book on circus-life straight from personal experience. He writes the honest kind of English which so often come from those who have a good memory, a good story to tell and no desire for false literary effect. (See also No. 72).

13. A FIGHT WITH A LION (*Missionary Travels*).

DAVID LIVINGSTONE (1813-1873) was the most famous of the nineteenth century British explorers and missionaries. The great virtue of his style is its honesty—the honesty of a true discoverer anxious above all to convey to his readers as plainly as possible the experiences which are new to them. Would this passage have been better if the writer had tried to make it more exciting, in the manner of a boys' adventure story?

14. A DOG FIGHT (*The Middle Aged Man on the Flying Trapeze*).

JAMES THURBER (born 1894) is one of the best known and most popular of modern American humorists. He illustrates his own books in a style as apparently simple and artless as his prose. But not many modern Americans are really simple and artless; Thurber's style, with its Americanisms and its conversational ease, is not easy to imitate successfully.

15. THAT THERE DOG O' MINE (*While the Billy Boils* First Series).

HENRY LAWSON (born 1875), a modern Australian short story writer tells of humble and unlucky people on the rougher side of Australian life. Notice how much is told us in less than a thousand words; or notice, rather, how much is left out. The point of the story is the sincerity and natural eloquence of an uneducated man under the influence of strong emotion, and the effect of his eloquence on the staff of the hospital. Lawson's economy of words is something that might well be imitated by other story writers.

16. THE KING OF THE CATS (*Journal at Geneva*).

PERCY BYSSHE SHELLEY (1792-1822) is known almost entirely by his poems, but he wrote also a considerable amount of prose, including some Journals of his travels in Europe. In this extract he recounts a brief "ghost" story told to him by an acquaintance. Is the style sufficiently simple for the story? (A longer extract from Shelley's Journals is *A Visit to Vesuvius*, No. 27).

17. A TRIAL FOR WITCHCRAFT (*Life of Sir Francis North*).

ROGER NORTH (1653-1734) was a brother of Sir Francis North, the Lord Keeper under Charles II and James II. He was a barrister, an M.P. and a country gentleman of varied tastes. He wrote books about fish and about music as well as politics and the history of his family. (Compare Evelyn, No. 4).

18. SIR LANCELOT AND THE FOUR KNIGHTS (*Le Morte Darthur*).

SIR THOMAS MALORY (died 1471) adapted and translated a mass of medieval legend about King Arthur and his knights, and his Morte Darthur is one of the greatest of English stories. It is a pity it is not more widely read. The language, now 500 years old, is in places strange to us, but a reader who has never enjoyed some at least of Malory's work in the original has missed a precious experience. "The pictorial power, the steady glow of chivalrous feeling throughout, the noble morality . . . . . the kindliness, the sense of humour, the melancholy and yet never either gloomy or puling sense of the inevitable end—all these are eminent in it." (Saintsbury).

19. DAVID COPPERFIELD'S DINNER (*David Copperfield*).

CHARLES DICKENS (1812-1870) was one of the greatest and best loved story writers of the Victorian age. He was born of humble parents near Portsmouth, and after an early life of hardship and struggle, much of which is described in *David Copperfield*, he became a journalist and so entered the world of literature. Purely as style, Dickens' prose is not always good; it is too often journalistic. But his manner of reporting conversation so as to bring out the maximum amount of humour and pathos is unrivalled. The way in which David's extreme simplicity and the waiter's cheerful rascality combine to produce this delightful situation shows the hand of a great humorist—one who knows how to divide the reader's heart between sympathy on the one hand and admiration on the other.

20. PATRONAGE (A Letter to Lord Chesterfield, from Boswell's *Life of Doctor Johnson*).

SAMUEL JOHNSON (1709-1784) was the son of a Lichfield bookseller. After a life of struggle against poverty and bad health he achieved a high literary reputation and was buried in Westminster Abbey. Some account of his difficulties, and of the patronage system, will be found in the next passage (No. 21) by Macaulay. After years of effort he produced in 1755 the first English Dictionary. He had sought in vain the help of Lord Chesterfield, a wealthy patron of the arts, and when the dictionary was completed, he was surprised to read some flattering articles about it by his lordship. This letter is Johnson's answer. His dignified and manly expression of hurt pride is well worth study because of its mastery of the means of giving the greatest possible force to each point. No-one would write a letter like this to-day, but a highly balanced and artificial style was more acceptable in Johnson's day. Do you think Johnson enjoyed writing it? For an example of Lord Chesterfield's writing, see No. 89.

21. LITERATURE IN DR. JOHNSON'S TIME (From an article in *The Encyclopaedia Britannica*).

THOMAS BABINGTON MACAULAY (1800-1859) was a scholar, a historian, and an M.P. His literary style is a model of clarity and force; he never reveals the slightest difficulty in making his meaning immediately intelligible to the reader. He avoids all vagueness of thought and expression and strives to make even abstract ideas as concrete as possible. Notice how in the latter half of this paragraph he reduces the idea of utter poverty to a series of vivid and memorable illustrations.

22. A VALLEY IN ABYSSINIA (*Rasselas*).

SAMUEL JOHNSON: see note on No. 20, p. 154. Johnson's description of a scene in Abyssinia is pure fantasy: he is not in the least concerned with geographical reality, as is the writer of the next description (compare No. 23). Johnson is describing a scene which exists only in his own mind, and he does so in elegant, balanced and highly artificial prose. Notice how nearly all the thoughts and images occur either in pairs or in threes. It is easy to criticise this style as unnatural and monotonous, but it has something of the charm of musical composition, and gains much from being read aloud.

23. LAKE TANGANYIKA (*The Lake Regions of Central Africa*).

SIR RICHARD FRANCIS BURTON (1821-1890) spent several years as an officer in the Indian Army, and later travelled in the Middle East and East Africa. His most famous book was his translation of the *Arabian Nights*. He writes with all the care and skill of an explorer determined above all to make as clear as possible to his readers scenes which they have never witnessed themselves. In this passage he is conscious of describing a view which no white man was recorded ever to have seen before.

24. FOG IN LONDON (*Nicholas Nickleby*).

CHARLES DICKENS: see note to No. 19, p.154.

This passage is a short sample of Dickens' mastery of "atmosphere"—the power of creating by the careful accumulation of detail a scene which any reader can recognise as real. Compare the famous second chapter of *A Tale of Two Cities*.

25. LONDON FOGS (*Essays and Sketches*).

CHARLES LAMB (1775-1834) was by profession a clerk in a London office and by choice a poet, playwright and essayist. His best known and best loved book, *Essays of Elia*, has found many imitators, but Lamb's style is impossible to imitate successfully because it is so intensely personal. Lamb's personality emerges from almost every sentence. In this passage he is determined to be cheerful and facetious, and to extract amusement even from something as depressing as a London fog. Compare his treatment of the subject with Dickens'.

26. A STONE AVALANCHE (*Mountaineering in 1861*).

JOHN TYNDALL: see note to Nos. 6 and 7, p.151.

The scientist here writes in a more dramatic and colourful style than elsewhere. Notice his use of metaphors and similes, which is as if a purely scientific style were inadequate to convey the tremendous effect he is describing.

27. A VISIT TO VESUVIUS (From a *Letter to Peacock*).

PERCY BYSSHE SHELLEY: see note to No. 16, p.153.

Shelley's imagery here has some of the vividness, force and rhetoric of his poetic writing. Compare for instance the end of the second stanza of the *Ode to the West Wind*:

Thou dirge
Of the dying year, to which this closing night
Will be the dome of a vast sepulchre,
Vaulted with all the congregated might
Of vapours from whose solid atmosphere
Black rain, and fire, and hail will burst:
O, hear!

28. AN ERUPTION OF VESUVIUS (*Arabia Deserta*).

CHARLES M. DOUGHTY (1843-1926) was interested above all in restoring to the English language the vigour and picturesqueness which he believed it had lost since the time of the Tudors. His *Arabia Deserta*, first published in 1888, has been called the greatest of all English travel books. He travelled, not for purposes of scientific discovery, but in order to write a great book as a means of reforming English style. By the sheer force and originality of his writing he attempts to make the reader share his own experiences directly. Consider to what extent he succeeds in this extract.

29. AN EARTHQUAKE (*Count Belisarius*).

ROBERT GRAVES (born 1895) is a poet and a writer of historical novels. This passage, unlike the two previous ones (Nos. 27 and 28), describes not an actual experience of the writer's, but an historical event as it might have appeared to an eye-witness. Notice the careful choice of adjectives to give as vivid a picture as possible, the dramatic use of short sentences to express the excitement of the event, and the skill with which the emotions of the servant who is describing it are shown to succeed one another in his mind. *The Reader Over Your Shoulder*, by Robert Graves and Alan Hodge, is the most exhaustive and penetrating study of English style that has been published in recent times.

30. WINTER ON SPITZBERGEN.

31. THE SILENT HAVEN (*Letters From High Latitudes*).

LORD DUFFERIN (1826-1902) wrote a series of letters to his mother to describe his travels in the Arctic in 1856 and 1857. The whole book is fascinating both for the interest of its material and for the vividness and humour of its descriptions of Arctic life and scenery. Two brilliant little impressions are given here—the first of intense cold, the second of intense stillness. It is worth while studying them to see how their effects are produced. The absence of superfluous words has something to do with it. (Compare '*The Great Frost*,' No. 5)

32. A DESERTED HOUSE (*To the Lighthouse*).

VIRGINIA WOOLF: see note on No. 5, p. 150.

AN extremely skilfully composed description, notable (like No. 30) for its lack of descriptive adjectives. The whole effect is built up by a careful selection of images suggesting neglect and disorder.

33. THE GOOSEBERRY BUSH (*The Herbal*).

JOHN GERARD (1545-1612) was an Elizabethan botanist, who compiled one of the first gardening books in English. Some things change little in three and a half centuries and the gooseberry bush seems to have changed less than the language in which Gerard describes it. His description is a model of clear writing and logical order: notice how he proceeds from general statements to the details of branch, leaf, flower, seed and root. This is the proper way to tackle scientific description.

34. DAFFODILS *from the Journal of*

DOROTHY WORDSWORTH (1771-1855). Compare this description with the preceding one. In what way does Dorothy Wordsworth's *purpose* in describing the daffodils differ from Gerard's purpose in describing the gooseberry? How does this difference affect their methods? Compare also the well-known poem by Dorothy's brother, William, inspired by the same experience.

35. THE CROCODILE (*Bartholomew*).

JOHN DE TREVISA (1326-1412) was a Cornish translator who wrote in English at a time when it was almost an adventure to do so. His description of the crocodile is now little more than quaint, and is included here for the sake of comparision with later scientific writers (e.g. Gilbert White, No. 40, and Darwin, Nos. 36, 37). The medieval writers were not 'scientific' in the modern sense, for factual accuracy was not their aim. They simply wrote down everything that was known or believed about their subjects, generally by classical authors, and did not trouble about personal observation or verification.

36. LAND LIZARDS OF THE GALAPAGOS ISLANDS.

37. LOCUSTS IN ARGENTINA (*The Voyage of the Beagle*).

CHARLES ROBERT DARWIN (1809-1882) was naturalist to a scientific expedition to the South Seas in H.M.S. *Beagle* from 1831 to 1836. His account of the voyage is one of the most delightful and fascinating books of natural history ever written. In literary as distinct from scientific achievement, according to Saintsbury, 'Darwin seems to have sought little, but he obtained something—an absolute clearness, a kind of competency and sufficiency for his own needs, which can never pass unnoticed.'

38. A TROPICAL FOREST.

39. NIGHT IN CENTRAL AMERICA (*A Naturalist in Nicaragua*).

THOMAS BELT (1832-1878) was a mining engineer who travelled to Australia, Nova Scotia and South America. His writings as a naturalist were admired by Charles Darwin.

The literary value of his work depends on his having felt the wonder and beauty of fresh scenes and acquired the skill necessary to convey those feelings in words. Compare his style with Darwin's (Nos. 36, 37). In the second extract by Belt, *Night in Central America*, in what way are the last lines, beginning 'The night speeds on . . . . ,' markedly inferior to the rest?

40. HOMING ROOKS (*The Natural History of Selborne*).

GILBERT WHITE (1720-1793) was a Hampshire parson who spent much of his leisure observing and describing the wild creatures of his native countryside. He had the true scientist's attitude—the habit of seeing accurately and patiently, of studying intelligently the theories of others, and of basing his own theories partly on the available evidence, partly on imagination. But White's book is more than a scientific treatise—it has inexhaustible charm and is pervaded with an almost poetic sense of peace and harmony with nature. His absolutely plain, unpretentious style is a model of what scientific and documentary writing should be; his observation is always sensitive and his touch delicate, yet he never seems to be striving after literary distinction by adopting a showy manner of expression or a dogmatic tone.

41. PIGEONS (*Cottage Economy*).

WILLIAM COBBETT: see note on No. 9, p.151 *Cottage Economy* was a little book of instruction for smallholders in the country. It is practical, sensible and written with great simplicity. Notice how even a 'practical' man was able to see the value of something which brought no immediate profit, and gave as the first 'use' of pigeons the fact that they are 'very pretty creatures.'

42. MOBY DICK (*Moby Dick*).

HERMAN MELVILLE (1819-1891) was born in New York. He had a restless, dissatisfied nature, and after trying several trades ran away to sea and served before the mast. It was not until after his death that he was recognised as one of the most original writers of sea stories who have ever lived. Melville's style is far from elegant and is full of clumsy constructions and old-fashioned expressions. But it is a powerful style, here well suited to its subject. In spite of being by no means easy to read, does not this passage make the reader feel the strength and malignancy of the dreaded white whale?

43. SIR ANDREW FREEPORT (*The Spectator*).
SIR RICHARD STEELE (1672-1729).

44. SIR ROGER AT CHURCH (*The De Coverley Papers*).

JOSEPH ADDISON (1672-1719). Steele and Addison were born in the same year and went to the same school. Steele founded one of the first newspapers, *The Tatler*, and he and Addison soon afterwards collaborated in editing *The Spectator*. Sir Andrew Freeport, like Sir Roger de Coverley, was a character invented by Steele. He was a typical Whig 'free-trader.' Addison wrote most of the essays about Sir Roger, who, though a typical country squire of the period, was an individual as well as a type. Steele and Addison set the tone for the eighteenth century, not only in manners, but also in literary style. Elegance, good taste, common sense, shrewd and penetrating humour are some of the qualities that made Addison in his time and for many years after it the most widely read of all prose authors. Dr.Johnson did not always display these qualities himself, but he was able to appreciate them in Addison. (See No. 103, p.178)

45. PARSON TRULLIBER (*Joseph Andrews*).

HENRY FIELDING (1707-1754) was a writer of plays and novels, a political pamphleteer and a London magistrate. His writing is full of satire, and much of what he did as well as what he wrote was a protest against the ills and weaknesses of eighteenth century society. A comparison of this portrait with the preceding one (No. 44, *De Coverley Papers*) will show that while Addison was mainly an observer, though a keen one, Fielding was a critic and a reformer. He is here describing a type of whom he fiercely disapproved—the lax and boorish country parson of his time. (Compare also No. 11, *A Walk to Salisbury*).

46. CORTEZ (*The Conquest of Mexico*).

WILLIAM HICKLING PRESCOTT (1796-1859) was an American historian. This passage gives not an intimate portrait, but a masterly summing-up in a single paragraph of a historical character. This is the true historian's gift—to be able, where necessary, to say much in a few lines, as some great painters can suggest miles of space in a few square inches of canvas.

47. THE DUKE OF MEDINA SIDONIA (*English Seamen in the XVIth Century*).

JAMES ANTHONY FROUDE (1818-1894) was an Oxford historian. This paragraph sums up the character and qualifications—or lack of qualifications—of the leader of the famous Armada. It is only half the length of the preceding one (No. 46, *Cortes*), but in one way it tells us more; the homely mention of orange gardens and sea-sickness suggest a real man as well as a historical figure.

48. A JAILER (*My Jailers*).

JAMES HENRY LEIGH HUNT (1784-1859) edited several journals and published many essays. He was imprisoned for attacking the Prince Regent in one of his periodicals. This passage shows his familiar, lively style at its best, and his gift for putting on paper the appearance, the mannerisms and even the accent of a character which has impressed itself on his memory.

49. THE PRISON GOVERNOR (*The Bible in Spain*).

GEORGE BORROW (1803-1881) travelled widely in Europe, sometimes as an agent of the British and Foreign Bible Society. It is possible to forget oneself more completely in his odd, rambling stories of gypsies, rogues and wanderers than in any other travel books in the language. Anything or anybody unconventional or out-of-the-way had an immediate fascination for him. His style is sometimes clumsy and awkward, but at its best it is the perfect medium for his strange and often grotesque reminisences. *The Bible in Spain* is packed with queer encounters and odd characters. Spain, as Borrow saw it, is a land of violent contrasts—brutality and kindness, grandeur and poverty, dignity and meanness, humour and sadness, brilliant sunshine and deep shadows. The contrast between the prison governor's courtly manner and his low character is typical.

50. MRS. BATTLE (*Essays of Elia*).

CHARLES LAMB: see note on No. 25, p. 156.
Several satirical portraits have been given in this section; here is a portrait drawn entirely from admiration. Lamb's style is not as a rule suitable for imitation—it is too personal and too mannered—but here it is more straightforward than usual; the portrait is well-proportioned and as Hazlitt says, drawn with a 'firm yet subtle pencil.'

51. MR. AND MRS. BENNET (*Pride and Prejudice*).

52. SIR JOHN AND LADY MIDDLETON (*Sense and Sensibility*).

JANE AUSTEN (1775-1817) lived what we should now consider an uneventful life, mainly in Hampshire and at Bath, the most fashionable health-resort of the eighteenth century (see No. 53). Her chief novels, based on experience of a very limited social circle engaged mainly in trivial occupations, are all master-pieces unrivalled in subtle character drawing and keen yet delicate irony. Her novels fascinate not because of the stories they tell, but because of their inexhaustible comedy of manners and personality. One of the novelist's finest gifts is the capacity to suggest character by dialogue. Jane Austen never gives a long descriptive analysis of her characters; she lets them talk—quite naturally, after the fashion of her day—and they reveal themselves to us, apparently without any help from the author. She always gives us, therefore, the delight of discovering their personalities for ourselves. How much do the two married couples in these passages reveal to us about themselves? Notice how the final paragraph in No. 54 scarcely does more than sum up what we have already learnt.

53. SOCIETY AT BATH.

54. BATHING MACHINES (*Humphrey Clinker*).

TOBIAS GEORGE SMOLLETT (1721-1771) was a Scottish surgeon and novelist. His writing is often coarse and his satire brutal, like the society he describes. His character-drawing, compared with Jane Austen's (Nos. 54, 56) is often caricature. Jane Austen produces her effects by understatement, Smollett by exaggeration.

55. A CRY OF FIRE (*from a letter*).

WILLIAM COWPER (1731-1800), poet, was the writer of a series of letters to his friends notable for their revelation of Cowper's own sensitive, humorous and rather fussy personality and for the insight they give us into English country life in the latter part of the 18th century. Cowper was an excellent reporter, and this description of a fire at Olney brings vividly before us the alarm and confusion, as well as the humour, of the incident. What interested Cowper, as an observer of this lively scene, was the behaviour of his fellow-townsmen. The letter from which this passage was taken was addressed to an evangelical clergyman. Hence, no doubt, the reference to Providence.

56. A CAIRO DRUGGIST.

57. ARRIVAL OF A CARAVAN (*A Pilgrimage to Mecca*).

SIR RICHARD FRANCIS BURTON: see note on No. 23, p. 156.

BURTON was one of the first Englishmen to make the pilgrimage to Mecca, the birthplace of Mahomet. It was so jealously guarded from the eyes of infidels that Burton was obliged to travel in disguise. This adds excitement to the intensely fascinating account he wrote of his journey. He possesses the indispensable gift for writing of this sort—the mind which records and stores picturesque or significant details, so that in No.57 the scene of bustle, glitter and confusion lives again as we read it.

58. A WRESTLING MATCH IN TAHITI (*The Journal*).

CAPTAIN JAMES COOK (1728-1779), the famous navigator, was, like Mungo Park (see Nos. 2, 65), killed by hostile savages. The story of his discoveries is admirably told in the plain, unpretentious prose of his journals. The style may seem rather 'prim' and dry to our ears, and a modern explorer would probably use a more racy vocabulary; but it is doubtful whether he would give a clearer or more faithful account. It is possible for a reader who has never seen anything at all like this wrestling match to visualise the whole thing with perfect ease.

59. DRY-FLY FISHING (*Fallodon Papers*).

EDWARD GREY, Viscount Grey of Fallodon (1862-1933) was Foreign Secretary at the outbreak of the Great War in 1914. This passage is included in the section on 'People' because it has to do with one of man's recreations. It is the great merit of Lord Grey's writings on fishing that he can make the subject interesting not only to anglers but also to those who have no interest in it as a pastime. Notice how the excitement of this placid recreation is conveyed; how the pace of the writing quickens after the intensely peaceful opening, and how the initial peacefulness is restored in the last few lines.

60. FIVE OF THE CLOCK (*The Fantasticks*).

NICHOLAS BRETON (1545?-1626?) was the author of numerous miscellaneous writings in verse and prose. This is an example of that admirable concrete writing of which there is such abundance in English, and which is so well worthy of study. There is scarcely a descriptive adjective or adverb in the whole passage and scarcely an abstract noun. Notice how vividly it conveys a sense of enjoyment, pleasure and satisfaction in the solid realities of a thriving countryside; and what a varied cross-section of Tudor society is represented in such a small space.

61. HARVESTING IN SCOTLAND (*A plan of the English Commerce*).

DANIEL DEFOE: see notes on No. 1, p.149 and No. 8, p.151. Besides *Robinson Crusoe* and other novels Defoe wrote many political phamphlets and books of what we should now call social study, of which his *Tour Through England and Wales* is the best known. He had at all times a lively interest in the conditions of labour. His observations are neither systematic nor scientific in the modern sense, but they are enlivened by humour and sturdy patriotic prejudice. His picture of the English labourer preferring puddings to music is perhaps not as flattering as Defoe intended it to be!

62. FELLING TREES (*Our Village*).

MARY RUSSELL MITFORD (1787-1855) wrote a novel, some plays, and many essays and sketches of life in a country town and village. The village so charming and faithfully described in the book from which this extract is taken is Three Mile Cross, near Reading in Berkshire. This description is the opposite of scientific, or 'objective,' writing, for the feelings of the writer enter into it at every stage. Notice how the feeling of sadness and a sense of loss, almost of tragedy, make themselves felt, even though the description is also faithful to life.

63, 64. HOP-PICKING (1) and (2) (*A Small Boy in The Sixties*).

GEORGE STURT (1863-1927) succeeded his father in the ownership of a wheelwright's business in Surrey, where farm carts and wagons of high quality were turned out by hand.

Sturt set himself to find out the reasons behind all the 'tricks of the trade' which constitute the wheelwright's hereditary skill. He wrote a book *The Wheelwright's Shop* to describe his discoveries. It is one of the most fascinating as well as one of the most clearly written books on craftsmanship that have ever appeared. He wrote several other books, mainly autobiographical, in which his principal concern was with the remains of hand-production and rural craft which persisted even in an age of increasing industrialisation. Sturt does not set up as a literary stylist; he is content to write prose which is faithful to the experiences he recalls, and which acquires thereby a fluency and grace of its own.

65. COOKING IN AFRICA (*Travels in the Interior of Africa*).

MUNGO PARK: see note on No. 2, p. 149.

66. MAIZE BREAD (*A Naturalist in Nicaragua*).

THOMAS BELT: see notes on Nos. 38, 39, p. 159.

67. PATAGONIAN GAUCHOS (*The Voyage of the Beagle*).

CHARLES DARWIN: see note on No. 36, 37, p. 159. In spite of one or two grammatical inaccuracies the style of this passage is in general graphic and unaffected. Notice how Darwin's sympathy with the horse is in conflict with his admiration of the man.

68. BEAR-HUNTING IN LAPLAND (*Letters from High Latitudes*).

LORD DUFFERIN: see notes on Nos. 30, 31, p. 158.

69. TRAVELLING IN THE DESERT (*A Pilgrimage to Mecca*).

SIR RICHARD BURTON: see notes on No. 23, p. 156 and Nos 56, 57, p. 164. The interest of this passage is mainly psychological: the writer describes, not so much a particular type of landscape as the state of mind produced by it. His style is more subtle, more personal and more metaphorical than that of some other nineteenth century travellers. At first sight the word order of the opening sentence does not seem quite satisfactory. Could it be improved?

70. KANO: A WEST AFRICAN CITY.

71. THE MARKET AT KANO (*Travels in Africa*).

CAPTAIN HUGH CLAPPERTON (1788-1827) was the son of a Scottish doctor, served in the navy, and later joined an expedition to explore the interior of Africa. On his second expedition he contracted a fever and died at Sokoto east of the river Niger. In describing Kano, the great trading centre to the south of the Sahara, which he was one of the first Europeans to visit, Clapperton's sole concern was to give an accurate, factual account of his observations.

72. LEARNED PIGS (*Seventy Years A Showman*).

'LORD' GEORGE SANGER: see note on No. 12, p. 152.

73. BEGGARS IN AMERICA (*The Adventures of Johnny Walker, Tramp*).

WILLIAM HENRY DAVIES (1871-1940) wrote many poems and several books of prose, mainly autobiographical. He went to the United States on a cattle boat, and for some years lived the rough, free life of an American beggar. He later begged in England, until he was able to scrape together enough money to devote his time to writing. His two books on the life of a tramp are among the most entertaining books ever written about an unconvential way of living. The style is simple and vivid, the narrative inconsequential and full of surprises. One of the chief attractions is Davies' odd, humorous observations on the many out-of-the-way characters he meets.

74. SUBJECTIVE COLOURS (*The Glaciers of the Alps*).

JOHN TYNDALL see note on No. 26, p. 156.

It is not easy to follow Tyndall's explanation of the phenomenon he observed in the Alps without paying close attention; nevertheless, he has succeeded in giving a clear and satisfactory account of it in a very short space. At first sight there is nothing in common between this passage and Sanger's *Learned Pigs* (No. 72) but the structure of the argument is in both cases the same. In the first paragraph the "mystery" is described and in the following paragraphs it is explained. Here the similiarity ends. It is worth considering, however, why and in what way Sanger's and Tyndall's styles are so different.

75. DEFORESTATION (*Earth and Man*).

E. N. DA C. ANDRADE (born 1887) is Professor of Physics, and JULIAN HUXLEY (born 1887) was for some time Professor of Zoology, at London University. Each is distinguished for his own work, and is a Fellow of the Royal Society and editor of the *Encyclopaedia Britannica* in his particular branch of science. But both have also taken pains to explain science simply and accurately to ordinary people. Huxley has always preferred to study animals outside the laboratory, and while Secretary at the London Zoo did much to make their surroundings as natural as possible. These two writers, in short, represent the new outlook, that scientists should be understandable and should in turn understand their own responsibility to society. The passage on *Deforestation* is typical of this outlook, in that it not only sets out in clear terms the scientific facts of deforestation, but it also points out its inescapable economic consequences.

76. THE LONDONER (*Essays and Sketches*).

CHARLES LAMB: see notes on Nos. 25, p.156, and 50, p. 163.

One reason why this passage is entertaining is that it is frankly personal in tone, making no pretence at impartiality. Lamb freely recognises that he is prejudiced. The story is therefore not objective and scientific; it is persuasive. One of the tricks of persuasive speech or writing is what is known as "begging the question"—that is, assuming that what you want to prove is true. If someone says to you, "What do you think of this hideous modern music?" the word "hideous" begs the question; the only possible answer is, "Well if it is hideous, there is no point in asking what I think of it". In the second paragraph of this extract Lamb uses two question-begging adjectives, "happy" and "silly". In spite of tricks like this, however, the passage contains serious arguments, which are worth considering.

77. WHY I COULD NEVER LIVE IN LONDON (*Hedge-Trimming*).

A. G. STREET (born 1892) is a farmer, journalist and broadcaster. The informal style of this passage is due to its being an extract from a broadcast talk. Like the previous extract, No. 76, it is personal and highly prejudiced, and is all the fresher for being so. Notice that Street dislikes London for much the same reasons as Lamb likes it. Even allowing for the differences between London as it is now and London as it was 150 years ago, it is clear that the opposing views of the two writers owe much to their differing temperaments. Behind the humour and exaggerations of Street's writing, there is a background of serious argument. Do you feel that either Lamb or Street is being strictly fair? and do you think strictly fair arguments make the most entertaining reading? When in your own essays you express personal opinions, try to do so as decidedly as you can. The secret of both Lamb's and Street's success is that they know their minds and state them boldly.

78. WALKING TOURS (*Virginibus Puerisque*).

ROBERT LOUIS STEVENSON (1850-1894) was a Scottish novelist, essayist and poet who combined chronic ill-health with an unfailing zest for life. His essays, from which this extract and also No. 96 are taken, show the energy of his mind and the ease and fluency of his style. Stevenson was very conscious of the sound-qualities of English, and he strove always to make his writing rhythmic and musical. There is no obscurity in Stevenson; he always says what he wants to say. He writes essays with the emphasis and persuasiveness of a good debater.

79. GOING FOR A WALK (*And Even Now*).

MAX BEERBOHM (b. 1872) is an essayist and a caricaturist. His satire is always keen but also kindly; it has a sort of friendly malice which always amuses and could scarcely hurt. His style is elegant and polished, yet it never appears affected because Beerbohm has an elegant and polished mind.

80. THE MISFORTUNES OF OTHERS (*Of the Sublime and Beautiful*).

EDMUND BURKE (1729-1797) was the son of an Irish lawyer and was educated in Dublin. He became an M.P., and the most brilliant and eloquent political writer of his time. His intellectual power was admitted and admired even by his enemies. His speeches on the American situation which culminated in the War of Independence are among the wisest and most humane ever made in Parliament. Hazlitt wrote of Burke: "It has always seemed to me that the most perfect prose-style, the most powerful, the most dazzling, the most daring, that which went nearest to the verge of poetry, and yet never fell over, was Burke's. It has the solidity, and sparkling effect of the diamond; all other *fine writing* is like French paste or Bristol stones in comparison." Burke is not easy or light reading, but he is worth the effort. His is certainly no style to imitate nowadays (except perhaps for a great speaker on a great occasion—some of Winston Churchill's broadcasts during the Second World War had the ring of Burke's eloquence) yet there is much to be learned from studying what Johnson called "his stream of mind".

81. PRISONERS (*The State of the Prisons*).

JOHN HOWARD (1726-1790) was apprenticed to a grocer, but on the death of his father, a well-to-do upholsterer, he gave up business and settled down to the quiet life of a country gentleman. When he became Sheriff of Bedford, he began to find out something of the appalling condition of the prisons. The rest of his life was devoted to improving these conditions by getting the facts widely known and arousing the conscience of his comfortable and easy-going contemporaries. This required great physical and moral courage, especially for a man of poor health like Howard. Even to go among prisoners meant the possibility of catching a deadly infection. Howard's observations and conclusions were published in 1777 and aroused widespread interest. This extract shows the breadth and humanity of his views, which even to-day are not universally accepted. At any rate the argument about "young delinquents" in the first paragraph is still often repeated. It is of a humanitarian such as Howard that we are thinking when we say that a man was "before his time".

82. THE WAR OF JENKINS' EAR (*Essay on Horace Walpole*).

THOMAS BABINGTON MACAULAY: see note on No. 21, p.155

In order to appreciate the force of Macaulay's style, it would be helpful to read this passage aloud. Notice how naturally the emphasis falls on the words which the sense requires to be emphasised; and how variety and interest are maintained by mixing long and short sentences. In spite of the apparent ease of Macaulay's style it is only a master of writing who can achieve such clarity. Macaulay is not profound or subtle, but what he wants to say he says with unerring skill.

83. THE EFFECTS OF PARTY GOVERNMENT (*A Vindication of Natural Society*).

EDMUND BURKE: see note on No. 80, p.171.

84. FREEDOM (*Speech to the Italian People, August* 1944).

WINSTON LEONARD SPENCER CHURCHILL (born 1874): soldier, journalist, politician, biographer, and Prime Minister from 1940 to 1945, during the greater part of the second World War. The Italian Fascist Government had declared war on Britain and France in 1940, and by 1944 had been driven out of the war, and destroyed. The British Prime Minister visited Italy while the troops of the United Nations were engaged in driving the Germans out of the country. He had always distinguished the Italian people from their Government, and before leaving the country he gave a speech of friendly encouragement and counsel to the Italian people in Rome. In the extract here given, he warned them of the dangers of tyranny and enumerated some simple tests by which it is possible to judge whether or not a nation has freedom.

These are memorable words, remarkable both for their simplicity and for their wisdom. We often speak of Freedom in the abstract, but without always knowing just what it is. Notice that Churchill does not answer that question directly, but states in a very definite and concrete manner how the presence or absence of Freedom can be detected. A modern orator unlike Burke cannot address himself to a limited audience of highly educated people; it is Churchill's distinction that many of his war speeches were admired and applauded both by the highly educated and by the poorly educated.

85. COVETOUSNESS (*from a Sermon*).

HUGH LATIMER (1485?-1555?) was the son of a yeoman farmer, took holy orders and became one of the leading preachers and churchmen of his time. He was condemned for heresy and burnt at Oxford during the reign of Queen Mary. His style is vivid and homely, and though always earnest it is full of amusing and ironical comments. His arguments combine a certain slow doggedness of mind with a shrewd wit and a deep-rooted honesty and tenacity of purpose often found among countrymen.

86. RAILWAYS (*Fors Clavigera*).

JOHN RUSKIN (1819-1900) was the son of a wine merchant, went to Oxford and became a writer on art, economics and social reform. He never ceased to question the motives and purposes behind industrial progress, and this short passage is his well-known denunciation of what he considered the purposeless destruction of natural beauty. Its style is ornate and rhetorical; its tone one of scornful anger. Is the argument fair?

87. WHY THE PYRAMIDS ? (*Rasselas*).

SAMUEL JOHNSON: see notes on Nos. 20, p. 154, and 22, p.155.

88. THE PYRAMIDS (*Eothen*).

ALEXANDER WILLIAM KINGLAKE (1809-1891) was the historian of the Crimean War and the author of *Eothen*, an account of his travels in the near East. Kinglake writes from the point of view of the amateur traveller, not the scientist, the missionary or the explorer; he took with him on his travels two assets, a sense of curiosity and a sense of humour, and these qualities made *Eothen* one of the most delightful of all travel books.

89. LAUGHTER (*Letters to his Son*).

LORD CHESTERFIELD (1694-1773) was a diplomat and a patron of the arts; he was the writer of a series of letters instructing his son in the principles of good breeding according to the notions of that period. By modern standards Chesterfield was a snob and a cynic, but he was also a man of sense, intelligence and even sensibility. (See also Johnson's famous letter, No. 20.)

90. CANT (Boswell's *Life of Dr. Johnson*).

SAMUEL JOHNSON: see notes on Nos. 20, p. 154, and 22, p.155

Johnson's famous exhortation, "Clear your mind of cant", is no less necessary to-day than it was when he made it. He is urging us to think for ourselves, and not to accept "ready-made" ideas which have become familiar through constant repetition. A thing is not necessarily true just because we read it in the newspapers or hear it said on the public platforms.

91. HONOUR (*Henry IV Part I*).

WILLIAM SHAKESPEARE (1564-1616) wrote dramatic prose of very high quality, but he does not seem to have esteemed it very highly, for he reserved it mainly for the use of servants, clowns and people in a state of mental disorder. Most of the Falstaff scenes in the two parts of *Henry IV* are written in a beautiful, rhymical prose which seems to have the ring of everyday Tudor speech. Wit and life are embodied in the very phrases which compose it. Here Falstaff is arguing himself into a cowardly course of action by maintaining that honour, which would spur him on in the battle, is only a word and therefore has no reality. To Falstaff, in fact honour is mere cant. Do you agree that this is a "trim reckoning"—that is, a neat argument?

92. A DUEL (*The Rivals*).

RICHARD BRINSLEY SHERIDAN (1751-1816) was the most brilliant and successful writer of comedies writing for the English stage during the greater part of the eighteenth century. By the time he was 30 he had given up writing plays and gone into Parliament. The arguments against honour put forward by Sheridan's David in this passage undoubtedly owe something to Falstaff, just as his most famous character, Mrs. Malaprop, owes much to Shakespeare's Dogberry in *Much Ado About Nothing*. (Compare No. 91)

93. GOING TO CHURCH (a Sermon).

HUGH LATIMER: see note on No. 85, p. 173.

94. RELIGION AND THE INDUSTRIAL REVOLUTION (*The Town Labourer* 1760-1832).

JOHN LAWRENCE HAMMOND (born 1872) and BARBARA HAMMOND (born 1873) wrote the sort of social and economic history which is an indispensable aid to the study of art and literature. *The Town Labourer* and *The Village Labourer* are classics of their kind. There are in this selection several authors of the period from Johnson to Macaulay (for instance, Howard, Burke, Cobbett and Jane Austen) whose writings would be greatly illuminated by reading the Hammonds' two great books. Not only is the matter of these books intensely interesting, it is described and commented on in a manner impossible to misunderstand. The style represents modern expository prose at its best, free from affectation, over-emphasis and looseness of thought or argument.

95. HAPPINESS (*Cottage Economy*).

WILLIAM COBBETT: see notes on Nos. 9, p. 151, and 41 ,p. 160.

Hazlitt said of Cobbett: "He is not only unquestionably the most powerful political writer of the present day, but one of the best writers in the language. He speaks and thinks plain, broad, downright English. He might be said to have the clearness of Swift, the naturalness of Defoe, and the picturesque satirical description of Mandeville; if all such comparisons were not impertinent. A really great and original writer is like nobody but himself." (*Table Talk.*) Read this extract from Cobbett in conjunction with the previous one (No. 94). Which of the Hammonds' "two contrary conclusions" would Cobbett have supported?

96. DEAD-ALIVE PEOPLE (*Virginibus Puerisque*).

ROBERT LOUIS STEVENSON: see note on No. 78, p. 170.

97. TOWNS AND THE INDUSTRIAL REVOLUTION (*The Town Labourer*, 1760-1832).

J. L. HAMMOND and BARBARA HAMMOND: see note on No. 94, p. 175.

98. RICH AND POOR (*A Vindication of Natural Society*).

EDMUND BURKE: see note on No. 80, p. 171.

This passage is the writing of a young man and is, for Burke, surprisingly radical—or as we should say, socialist—in tone. It was a very different Burke who thirty years later wrote against the French Revolution and was attacked by the radical, Tom Paine.

99. A NATURAL ARISTOCRACY (*An Appeal from the New to the Old Whigs*).

EDMUND BURKE: see notes on Nos. 80, p. 171, and 176.

Here is an example of the later Burke, writing during the French Revolution, an event which deeply affected opinion in England; those of moderate views tended to become either more radical, or more conservative as Burke did. Burke considered the French Revolution to be a terrible example of what might happen in a country where the principle of hereditary aristocracy was attacked.

100. POETRY AND POLITICS (*The Dedication to the Examen Poeticum*).

101. CHAUCER (*The Preface to Fables*).

JOHN DRYDEN (1631-1700), poet, dramatist and critic, was perhaps of all great writers the one whose genius it is most difficult to represent, either in prose or in verse, by short quotations. A glance at the chronological index to this book will help to explain Dryden's position. There had been good prose before his time, but it is not modern, it is not the English of to-day; on the other hand, the major writers after Dryden—Addison, Swift, Fielding, Burke, and so on—all wrote a style which in some respects at least is recognisably modern. Dryden, almost alone, was responsible for the change. He consciously modernised the written English language, in order to be able to give adequate expression in prose to his views on drama and poetry. In doing so he was also the founder of systematic literary criticism in England.

The passage on *Chaucer* is an example of Dryden's literary criticism, than which none had yet appeared of greater breadth and humanity; the passage on *Poetry and Politics* shows Dryden fiercely asserting the dignity of a poet's calling in an age when all writers were dependant on aristocratic and political patronage. (Compare Macaulay, No. 21, and Johnson, No. 20.)

102. OF STUDIES (*Essays*).

FRANCIS BACON (1561-1626) was first Baron Verulam and Viscount St. Albans, but *not* "Lord Bacon", as he is often called. He was trained as a lawyer, entered Parliament, rose to be Lord Chancellor, sacrificed his entire public position by being convicted of corruption, spent a few days in the Tower and devoted the rest of his life to literary pursuits. He has been widely condemned for the leading part he took in the trial for treason of the Earl of Essex, who had generously helped Bacon in his earlier career. The truth is that Bacon was little worse and no better than many of his contemporaries in public life. The age was one in which it was difficult to rise except by more or less unscrupulous ways. If Bacon was really as mean as some of his actions, it is impossible to make sense of the wisdom and humanity of his writing. Bacon evidently had one of those complex personalities which make the Elizabethan period so baffling. Nowadays we are revolted by a man who talks with such wisdom and acts with such meanness, but a dual character of this sort neither surprised nor revolted the average Elizabethan.

Bacon's writing is remarkable chiefly for its compression of thought. The essay *Of Studies* contains enough material for a whole volume of literary criticism. The best way to appreciate this quality in Bacon's prose is to try to expand a few lines to their full meaning in modern English. Such a paraphrase would provide a valuable though exacting exercise in comprehension and expression.

103. ADDISON'S STYLE (*Lives of the Poets*).

SAMUEL JOHNSON: see notes on Nos. 20, p. 154; 22, p. 155, and 90, p.174.

Most of Johnson's literary criticism is contained in the *Lives of the Poets* which he wrote as prefaces to a collection of their works. He was a generous critic where he admired, but unduly severe where he had no sympathy.

104. ON FAMILIAR STYLE (*Table Talks*).

WILLIAM HAZLITT (1778-1830) was a political journalist, an essayist, and a critic of art and literature. He had an extremely acute critical sense and an irritable and prejudiced nature, a combination which makes his writing full of variety and interest. He was an unsystematic critic, and is notorious for his habit of misquotation; but he possesses more than most other critics the quality of zest, and this he never fails to convey to the reader. Do you agree with his estimate of Johnson's style?

105. STYLE (*Literary Taste*).

ENOCH ARNOLD BENNETT (1867-1931) was a journalist and novelist. His view of style, though an extreme one, and expressed dogmatically, is probably the only satisfactory one. We continually talk of matter and style as if they were separate and distinct; but ultimately they are inseparable from one another, as is the personality of the writer. "The Style is the thought" and "The Style is the man". That is why style is important.

INDEX OF REFERENCES

FOR THE STUDY OF PROSE COMPOSITION

(*The numbers given below refer to the numbers of the extracts*).

I. TYPES OF STYLE. (The list of passages given under each heading is not exhaustive; it indicates those passages in which certain main kinds of writing may best be studied).

(i) Plain or familiar.
1, 3, 8, 9, 10, 12, 13, 14, 18, 25, 29, 41, 50, 58, 61, 63, 70, 71, 72, 73, 79, 85, 93, 104, 105.

(ii) Formal or artificial.
5, 11, 16, 17, 20, 22, 23, 32, 46, 80, 87, 102.

(iii) Dialogue or direct speech.
9, 15, 19, 49, 51, 91, 92.

(iv) Impressionism.
5, 12, 23, 24, 29, 30, 31, 32, 34, 40, 59.

(v) Scientific, detached.
5, 6, 7, 30, 33, 36, 37, 65, 66, 74, 94.

(vi) Logical, persuasive.
21, 75, 78, 80, 81, 82, 84, 85, 96, 98, 99.

(vii) Rhetorical or emotional.
20, 26, 62, 76, 77, 83, 86, 89, 95, 100.

(viii) Passages of special interest for the study of vocabulary and stylistic devices.
5, 10, 18, 20, 22, 26, 28, 42, 69, 83, 102.

II. MEMORISATION. (The following passages are especially suitable for the selection of extracts to be learnt by heart.)
3, 10, 18, 20, 32, 60, 80, 83, 86, 90, 95.

III. Composition. (The following passages will be found among the most suitable for the type of exercise indicated.)

(i) General comprehension and oral discussion.
1, 6, 7, 13, 17, 18, 28, 36, 37, 41, 44, 48, 56, 63, 64, 69, 72, 74, 76, 81, 85, 94, 95, 97, 98, 102, 104, 105.

(ii) Paraphrase. (Parts of the following passages will be found suitable for paraphrase.)
4, 11, 17, 18, 33, 35, 85, 91, 93, 100, 102.

(iii) Summary or Precis.
Short or medium. 4, 16, 21, 41, 43, 45, 46, 54, 80, 82, 87, 88, 89, 94, 99, 105.
Longer. 2, 3, 7, 15, 27, 42, 50, 67, 69, 72, 74, 77, 81, 84.

(iv) Imitation and original composition. (The following suggestions are for exercises, or types of exercise, that might be attempted after reading the passages indicated by numbers below:

3 (a) An account in Swift's style of your reception on a strange planet.
(b) An account of his experiences written by the Lilliputian mentioned in the last sentence of the passage.

4, 5 A Heat Wave.

6 (a) A mountain walk
(b) A scramble on the cliffs.

8 (a) Captain Singleton at the village shop.
(b) Captain Singleton at a large department store.

10, 11 A modern story relating an act of charity.

12 (a) Fire on the farm.
(b) The city water-main bursts.
(c) The lights fail at the village concert.
(d) Animals break loose at the fair.

14, 15 (a) My dog.
(b) My neighbour's dog.
(c) A runaway horse.

16 (a) A short ghost story.
(b) A strange dream.

17 A practical joke.

18 (a) A football or hockey match in the style of Malory.
(b) Sir Lancelot carries his bat.

19 What do you learn from this passage about the character of David Copperfield?

20 (a) A letter in Dr. Johnson's style to the local newspaper on some topic of local or national interest.
(b) Dr. Johnson writes to the neighbours to complain of their wireless set.
(c) A letter to the local paper on the need for more playing-fields or for a swimming-bath.
(d) A short speech at the opening of a new Youth Club or at a school Speech Day.

21 (a) An incident in the life of any famous person told in your own words.
(b) Conditions in the navy at the time of Nelson.
(c) Conditions in factories during the Industrial Revolution.
(d) Life in the ideal school.

22, 23 How can you tell from these two passages that Johnson is describing an imaginary scene and Burton an actual one.

24, 25 (a) Compare Dickens' and Lamb's treatment of the same subject.
(b) Write a description of *either* Mist in the Country, *or* Fog at a sea-port.

26 (a) A hailstorm.
(b) A cloudburst.

27-29 Which of these three descriptions do you prefer, and why?

30-32 (a) Moonlit streets.
(b) A churchyard.
(c) A neglected garden.
(d) A Victorian parlour.
(e) A super-cinema.

33 (a) A tomato-plant as described by Gerard.
(b) A strawberry plant described in your own style.
34 (a) An impression of a bluebell wood.
(b) Compare this passage with Wordsworth's poem *The Daffodils.*
35-37 (a) A fox, as described by John of Trevisa.
(b) A crocodile, as described by a modern scientifiic writer.
(c) Cats.
38, 39 (a) Night on the farm.
(b) Night in the hills.
(c) In the botanical gardens (or ornamental park)
(d) A fir wood.
41 (a) The advantages of keeping rabbits, *or* collecting butterflies.
(b) "Go to the ant, thou sluggard."
43, 44 (a) A description in the 18th century style of *either* a doctor, *or* a dentist.
(b) A parson, *or* a lawyer, in modern English.
(c) A schoolmaster, *or* schoolmistress.
46, 47 The character of any famous statesman, soldier or sailor.
48, 49 (a) Compare Leigh Hunt's gaoler with Borrow's.
(b) A Welsh farmer.
(c) A Scottish gardener.
(d) A Cockney character.
(e) An old tramp.
51 (a) Show how the contrasting characters of Mr. and Mrs. Bennet are revealed in their conversation.
(b) Write a short dialogue illustrating two other characters, real or imaginary.
52 What does this passage tell us of the characters of Sir John and Lady Middleton?
56 (a) An antique-dealer.
(b) A match-seller.
(c) A snack-bar and its proprietor.

57 (a) A busy day at Woolworth's.
(b) A country fair.
(c) A street market.
(d) A barber's shop.
(e) A suburban railway station.

58 (a) A turn at the circus.
(b) A boxing match.
(c) An exciting event at the school sports.

60 (a) 8 a.m.—twentieth century, by Nicholas Breton.
(b) Early-closing day.
(c) 5 p.m. in the city.

62 (a) The departure of an express train.
(b) The launching of a ship.
(c) Demolishing an old building.

63, 64 (a) Potato-picking.
(b) Fruit-picking.
(c) Harvest.

65, 66 (a) Sunday dinner.
(b) Christmas pudding.
(c) Jam-making.

67 (a) Learning to swim.
(b) Learning to ride a bicycle.

69 A long journey by motor-coach.

70, 71 (a) My favourite village.
(b) The fish market.

73 (a) Street musicians.
(b) The U.S.A. according to the cinema.
(c) The detective in fiction and fact.

74 (a) How an electric torch works.
(b) How a photograph is made.
(c) How to work a sewing-machine.
(d) How an aeroplane flies.

75, 86 (a) The preservation of rural England.
(b) The roads of Britain.
(c) An internal system of air-transport for Britain.

76, 77 (a) Compare Lamb's and Street's arguments.
(b) Why I could never live in the country.

(c) The ideal broadcasting service.
(d) The pleasures of music.

103-105 (a) The characteristics of a good prose style.
(b) American slang.
(c) The style of *either* Johnson, *or* Defoe, *or* Dickens.
(d) The importance of writing well.
(e) "The chief glory of every people arises from its authors." (Johnson)
(f) "Home is the girl's prison and the woman's workhouse." (Shaw)
(g) "I would sooner have written *Alice in Wonderland* than the whole *Encyclopedia Britannica*." (Stephen Leacock)
(h) "The best part of every man's education is that which he gives to himself." (Scott)
(i) "No man but a blockhead ever wrote except for money." (Johnson)